An Ocean in Mind

An Ocean in Mind

WILL KYSELKA

A Kolowalu Book

UNIVERSITY OF HAWAII PRESS · HONOLULU

92 91 90 89 88 87   5 4 3 2 1

Library of Congress Cataloging-in-Publication Data

Kyselka, Will.
  An ocean in mind.

  (A Kolowalu book)
  Bibliography: p.
  Includes index.
  1. Navigation, Primitive—Polynesia. 2. Cognition
and culture. 3. Learning. 4. Hokule'a (Canoe)
I. Title.
GN670.K97 1987   910.4'5   87–19171
ISBN 0–8248–1112–7

To Dr. E. W. Haertig, psychiatrist, teacher, friend, whose work with Mary Kawena Pukui and Catherine A. Lee in Nānā i ke Kumu *[Look to the Source] illuminates ancient ways of being as expressed in* ʻohana *and in* hoʻoponopono.

And to the crews of Hōkūleʻa *who, in sailing forth in search of the mind of the Polynesian of old, found inseparable the joy of discovery and the benign indifference of the sea.*

CONTENTS

About this Book   ix

Convergence   3
In the Beginning   7
Polynesia—Watery World   11
Tahiti, 1976   17
Kealaikahiki   23
High Wind, High Hope   27
Stellar Clues   37
Journey by Starlight   47
Two Men, Two Ways   59
Into the Smoke   69
Increasing Momentum   73
Singapore Swing   83
Strategy   95
In Peril on the Sea   105
Waiting for the Wind   117
Stormy Weather   125
Halcyon Days   135
In and out of the Doldrums   151
Speeding over the Equator   165
Slowing down South   175
The Bounding Main   191
The Wayfinder   205
Perspective   223
The Blessing   235

Crew Members on *Hōkūleʻa,*
1976, 1977, 1978, 1980   237
For Further Reading   239
Index   241

ABOUT THIS BOOK

*F*or a long time I have been fascinated with how we think and how we learn. Over a period of two decades and more at the University of Hawaii Laboratory School in Honolulu I've been in touch with a variety of students and their various modes of learning—with those who learn in conventional ways and with those who must invent to know.

My purpose in writing this book is to describe a way of learning —the particular way in which Nainoa Thompson generated his own navigational knowledge in the Bishop Museum Planetarium, learned the ways of the sea from the master Carolinian navigator Mau Piailug, then integrated it all into a cogent wayfinding system uniquely his own that enabled him to find tiny islands over vast oceanic distances in the manner of the ancients, without instruments.

Nainoa and Mau are doers. My way of being is in writing about what I see happening. We three stand in a niche on the side of an old volcano watching the stars over the Moloka‘i Channel in the pre-dawn darkness of a winter solstice day. I stand behind the two, scrawling words in large hand on the pages of a speckle-covered composition notebook as we await the first streaks of light to reveal the prevailing wave patterns for the day.

Here in this trio of observers are three ways of learning, three ways of being. Each is dealing with his own range of experience vastly different from the others', and each is silently sorting sense data into the convenient cognitive bins of formula, metaphor, and measurement.

An Ocean in Mind is intended for the person interested in the process, curious about what it's like to get an ocean of information in mind, transform it into knowledge, and then trust mind and senses to find the way to distant lands.

Nainoa invented a way for finding islands. Rational and efficient, we wondered what to call it. Navigation is what it is—directing a vessel over the sea to an intended destination. However, since we generally think of navigation as involving the use of instruments, we switched to the term "non-instrument navigation." But that sounded condescending, and even "landfinding," incomplete. At the center of a circle of sea and sky is the navigator, trusting mind and senses within a cognitive structure to read and interpret nature's signs along the way as the means for maintaining continuous orientation over vast oceanic distances to remote, intended destinations. This is *human navigation*. We call it *wayfinding*.

Augmenting my views in this book are those of *Hōkūleʻa* crew members as they expressed them to the on-board documentor, Steve Somsen. He also interviewed Nainoa frequently, and excerpts from those dialogues are included. And in a chapter of his own Nainoa tells of that awesome "moment of self-perspective, of one person in a vast ocean given an opportunity of looking through a window into my heritage."

Such a privileged moment is possible only within a community committed to increasing our understanding of the art of wayfinding —from hundreds of friends and members of the Polynesian Voyaging Society, business organizations, and the legislature of the State of Hawaii.

I wish to thank the Board of Trustees of the Bernice P. Bishop Museum and Edward Creutz, director of the museum at that time, for making the planetarium available for navigational research; and George Bunton, who was manager of the planetarium and saw to it that this research in human navigation could begin; and to Walter Steiger, who maintains the momentum. Also thanks to Evelyn Klinckman, Victor Kobayashi, Victor Lipman, Beverly Creamer, Susan Ramos, Cary Sneider, Donna deHaan, and Betty Bushnell for suggestions; and to Arthur R. King, Jr., Frank Pottenger, and Loretta Krause for interpreting me to the university community.

Thanks to our friends in Tahiti: to Radio Mahina who talked us into the harbor at Papeʻete, to Harbor Director Lulu LaCaille who guided us to the pier, and Gerard Cowan who guided us through protocol, to the Tai Nui Canoe Club for their hospitality, and to the Tuamotuans who sang and danced for us at a *lūʻau*.

And thanks to the crew of the 1976 voyage—particularly Buffalo Keaulana, Boogie Kalama, and Billy Richards—who welcomed the 1980 crew with a *lūʻau* on the sands of Mākaha Beach in Waiʻanae, presenting us *maile* leis and affirming in that act a continuity in Polynesian voyaging after a hiatus of centuries.

Thanks also to Richard Gelwick whose book *Discovery* introduced me to the writings of Michael Polanyi; and to Jerome Bruner whose book *On Knowing: Essays for the Left Hand* is old and good and comfortable.

Illustrations in this book are by Ray Lanterman. His sky maps are from the Polynesian Voyaging Society's book *Polynesian Seafaring Heritage*. His meridional star charts are from the book *North Star to Southern Cross*. The second chapter, "In the Beginning," is one that I put together from various traditional sources and from a view of the sky within the planetarium. The chant, composed by Keliʻi Tauʻa, can be heard on Jack deMello's record album, *Hōkūleʻa*. And the term "wayfinding" is from the book by Downs and Stea, *Maps in Mind*. The photograph of Kawaiahaʻo churchyard is by Francis Haar; all other photos are the author's.

Distances throughout this book are expressed in English units, statute and nautical units as seems appropriate. The nautical mile conveniently relates angular and linear measure. One degree of longitude measured at the equator is equal to 60 nautical miles. One sixtieth of a degree is the nautical mile, equivalent to 1.15 statute miles or 1.85 kilometers. The knot is measure of speed, equivalent to one nautical mile per hour.

An Ocean in Mind

Convergence

*T*he moon came up in the wrong place.

That's how we met.

Or, more precisely, in 1977 as Nainoa was navigating *Hōkūleʻa* on the 350-mile Kealaikahiki research project, he saw the moon rising where he didn't expect it. Clearly, either he had made a discovery of uncommon proportion or his thinking was in error. Hoping for the former while suspecting the latter, he came to the Bernice Pauahi Bishop Museum Planetarium in Honolulu for an understanding which had eluded him on that unforgettable night at sea.

Here in the planetarium we ran time backward, back to that puzzling week in April of 1977. Planets, sun, and moon hummed in high pitch as their slurring motors hustled them across the sky and among the stars that shone brightly on the 30-foot dome.

Planetary motion slowed to a standstill as the "wanderers" took the places they had held on the afternoon of the first of April. Then we ran time slowly forward, watching not only the continuously changing relationship of sun and moon but also the dramatic shifting in the moon's rising and setting places as it completed a month of phases.

A gibbous, or "lopsided," moon began rising at four on that Friday afternoon, at just the same place on the horizon where the sun had appeared ten hours earlier. Waxing, the gibbous moon in two days would be full and then take its place near the bright blue star, Spica, in the constellation Virgo.

The following evening the moon rose an hour before sunset. That was no surprise. But what was surprising to Nainoa was that it rose south of where the sun had risen that morning. Why?

A Full Moon—a strange one—rose on Sunday evening. Ordinarily the Full Moon rises large and brilliant just as the sun sets. Not this moon. It was there all right, but not with its customary Full Moon brilliance. So quietly, in fact, did the faint moon slide onto the celestial scene that only the most avid lunar observer would have noticed it at all.

Why the dimly lighted disk? An hour earlier it had entered the earth's shadow; this evening it was rising eclipsed. Even though it was totally within the earth's shadow it was still visible, for sunlight, bent and filtered in its journey through the earth's atmosphere, was brightening the shadow with an uncommon coppery cast. Two hours after sunset the moon had moved out of the shadow and into the sunlight where once again it was restored to full brilliance.

An even stranger sight for Nainoa was moonrise on that Monday evening—an hour after sunset. Again that was no surprise, but what was surprising to him this time was that the moon rose several degrees south of where the sun had risen that morning. For this he was not prepared. It made no sense. He could not understand it.

But in the darkness of the planetarium, he could see in a flash what might have taken years of observing the sky to comprehend. He had expected the sun and the Full Moon to rise at the same point on the horizon; but he found that was not necessarily so. Sun and Full Moon are 180° apart; they take opposite positions in the sky. When the sun sets 4° north of west (as it does in early April), the Full Moon rises 4° south of east. Immediately he saw why the picture of the sun-moon relationship he had been carrying in his head did not fit the reality of the event he had witnessed on that most perplexing night at sea.

Neither of us said much. Perhaps it was shyness on both our parts. He was then a quiet young man of twenty-four; I a teacher thirty-two years his senior. He had always had an interest in the sea, and in 1976 experienced it in a new way, as a member of the crew on the return voyage of *Hōkūle'a*.

His interest in the sea was shaping his life; he knew what he was about. He must learn the stars and the sea and how to sail to distant islands as his Hawaiian ancestors had done. He came to the planetarium to learn the stars, and over a period of years we learned from each other.

I was impressed with his persistence: the way he searched for what he needed to know, integrating it all into a coherent structure. Over the next few years I saw him invent a geometry of necessity that by-passed mathematical formulae. Something there was in his nature and in mine that enabled us to work together for hundreds of hours relating stars in the sky to islands in the sea. Gradually I learned more about him, finding that he had scored off the top end of the so-called intelligence tests yet had barely squeaked through high school. And I saw him work ten years, somewhat casually, getting his bachelor's degree at the University of Hawaii.

Nainoa is a lithe, thin man, of half-Hawaiian ancestry. A lively curiosity and a deep affinity for the sea were powerful forces impelling him toward knowing his heritage. To know, he must risk. He chose to find kinship with the sea, to sail routes his ancestors had sailed centuries ago, to learn how they might have used the light of stars to guide them over this watery world.

Nainoa and Will at the starboard steering sweep; Henry Piailug in the background

In the Beginning

*L*ong, long ago—longer than anyone can remember or even imagine—there were no stars in the sky.

Sky was the god Wākea. Earth, the goddess Papa. Man and wife, they loved each other and held each other in tight embrace. The children of the gods, caught in the darkness between their parents, had very little room to move.

All was darkness. Cosmic darkness—*pō*.

The children longed to see the light so that they could know contrasts and distinguish substance from void. So oppressive then was Sky upon Earth that all the leaves on the trees were flattened—as they are still today.

"Let us destroy mother and father," said one young rebel god. "In that way we will be able to move about freely and attain our own identities."

But wiser heads prevailed. And it was the greatest of the young gods, Kāne, who said, "Let us instead separate Earth and Sky, mother and father, and in that way we will not have the burden of guilt in the death of our parents." A good plan to which all agreed, and one by one each would try.

First to go forth was mighty Kū. He had that confidence that comes in feeling himself equal to the task of separating Earth and Sky, and that he would be the bringer of light to the children of the gods.

Mighty Kū went forth heroically, placed his feet firmly against Earth goddess Papa, his hands firmly against Sky god Wākea. He took deep breaths and flexed his knees. Then at the moment that was right for him, Kū pressed upward against the sky. He trembled and shook under the burden of the heavens.

But try as he might, mighty Kū was unable to separate Earth and Sky, mother and father. All still was darkness.

Next to go forth was mighty Kanaloa. He had that confidence that comes in merely feeling himself superior in strength to brother

Kū, and that he would be the separator of Earth and Sky and the bringer of light to the children of the gods.

Kanaloa went forth heroically, placed his feet firmly against Earth goddess Papa, his hands firmly against Sky god Wākea. He thought great thoughts. He took deep breaths and flexed his knees. Then at the moment that was right for him, Kanaloa pressed upward against the sky. He trembled and shook under the burden of the heavens, sweated and strained.

But try as he might, mighty Kanaloa, like brother Kū, was unable to separate Earth and Sky, mother and father. All still was darkness.

Next to go forth was mighty Lono. He had that confidence that comes in feeling that the mantle of greatness would descend upon him, and that he would be the separator of Earth and Sky and the bringer of light to the children of the gods.

Lono went forth heroically, placed his feet firmly against Earth goddess Papa, his hands firmly against Sky god Wākea. He thought great thoughts and prayed great prayers. He took deep breaths and flexed his knees. Then at the moment that was right for him, Lono pressed upward against the sky. He trembled and shook under the burden of the heavens, sweated and strained, and grunted and groaned.

But try as he might, mighty Lono, like brothers Kanaloa and Kū, was unable to separate Earth and Sky, mother and father. All still was darkness.

At last the greatest of the young gods, Kāne, went forth, filled with a sense of manifest destiny that comes in knowing that he would be the separator of Earth and Sky and the bringer of light to the children of the gods.

Kāne went forth heroically, placed his feet firmly against Earth goddess Papa, his hands firmly against Sky god Wākea. He thought great thoughts, prayed great prayers, chanted great chants. He took deep breaths and flexed his knees. Then at the moment that was right for him, Kāne pressed upward against the sky. He trembled and shook under the burden of the heavens, sweated and strained, grunted and groaned—he pushed so hard that the veins stood out on the sides of his neck.

But try as he might, mighty Kāne, like brothers Lono, Kanaloa, and Kū, was unable to separate Earth and Sky, mother and father. All still was darkness.

"Why?" he wondered, "Why am I unable to perform this task?" He thought and thought and thought, then tried another way. He lay down on the ground, braced shoulders against Earth goddess Papa, his feet against Sky god Wākea. He trembled and shook, sweated and strained, grunted and groaned as he pressed upward against the sky. Slowly, very slowly Sky began separating from Earth. Light flooded in between the two. And there was darkness no more.

Delighted at last in seeing the light, the children of the gods began exploring. They explored far and wide. Hina, goddess of the moon, explored so far over the earth that she ended up in the sky. Often you can see her in the moon, sitting beneath a *hala* tree pounding out *kapa*. The *kapa* she hangs up to dry are the beautiful white clouds that hug the crests of the mountains.

The sun shone by day and the moon by night. But there were no stars in the sky.

Wākea, arched above, would cry and bemoan his fate, "What have we done to deserve so cruel a treatment from you, our children?" His tears of remorse are the warm, gentle rains that fall upon the islands. Earth goddess Papa shudders and sighs, and sobs and shakes, bemoaning her fate of separation. Those are the earthquakes that rock the islands. And her tears? The gentle mists that roll up into mountain valleys.

The children of the gods, seeing the body of their father Wākea above and unadorned, felt compassion. They picked up stars and placed them in a basket. From that basket they took the stars, one by one, and placed them in the heavens. They made the brightest star to travel over Tahiti, and they made blue-white Spica to travel over Samoa. And they left the basket in the heavens, too, a star group we know as Corona Borealis.

If bright stars mark important islands, then what islands must lie beneath the path of that bright star in the north, that star right off the curve of Nā-hiku, "the seven?" Important islands they must be, for also traveling over that island group is a "cluster of little eyes," Nā-huihui-a-Makaliʻi.

And so it may be that it was the stars that suggested to the children of old in their southern islands that land might lie to the north.

For the earth is ocean. And rising everywhere in it are islands. Go find the islands . . .

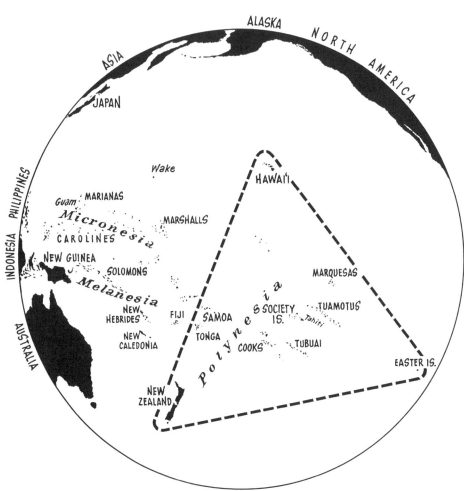

The Polynesian Triangle

Polynesia—Watery World

*T*he Pacific Ocean covers half the earth's surface. Between Singapore and Panama are 12,000 miles of ocean. Within this watery world are ten thousand islands, most of them tiny specks of land lying within the tropics—between the "turning places of the sun."

Islands near Asia are large and closely spaced. But with increasing distance from the continent they become smaller, more widely dispersed. So great is this eastward thinning that beyond Easter Island and Hawai'i is a 2,400-mile stretch of open ocean almost completely devoid of islands.

Islands in the western Pacific rest on the shallow continental shelf of Asia. Here on the western continental side of the Pacific basin are volcanoes of explosive nature, volcanoes that have built imposing cones such as Fujiyama in Japan and Mayon in the Philippines. But volcanoes within the Pacific basin are of gentle nature, building huge, dome-shaped mountains such as Mauna Kea and Mauna Loa.

Long periods of erosion gradually carved these volcanic giants into sharp ridges and deep valleys, leaving jagged peaks to mark their central cores. Both Hawai'i and Tahiti are high islands with rugged interior regions covered with vegetation lush and green.

Low islands are made of coral that grows on the truncated tops of former volcanic giants. Extend the arc of the Caroline Islands eastward through the Marshalls, Gilberts, Ellice, Tokelau, and Tuamotu islands and you include most of the coral islands in the Pacific. When seen from the air, the larger ones may look like huge sea creatures stretching over the water. Others are coral strips surrounding central lagoons, like beads on a necklace.

Oceania is a huge region of the Pacific encompassing three island groups: Micronesia, Melanesia, and Polynesia. Eastern Oceania is Polynesia, a triangular region of "many islands." Marking the corners of the Polynesian triangle are the islands of New Zealand, Easter Island, and Hawaiʻi. Within the triangle lives a people of common culture, common language, common appearance. Captain James Cook called it the "most extensive nation on earth." How was it possible for a people to settle so large a portion of this planet?

Were the Polynesians of old a people who, after setting forth in fragile canoes, were driven by wind and wave unknown distances to unknown islands and left there with little hope ever again of returning home? Or were they a hardy and venturesome people who, sailing forth in sturdy canoes of their own design, found remote islands and returned home to tell others of their discoveries?

THE SETTLING OF POLYNESIA—TWO VIEWS

Two points of view are held on the settling of Polynesia. One argues that it was accidental; the other, intentional.

The accidental voyaging hypothesis holds that the Polynesians of old had neither the navigational skills nor vessels capable of reaching remote islands. So if they got there it must have been by accident.

Later, that concept was enlarged to include one-way voyaging, allowing that if, indeed, the people had vessels capable of long-distance voyaging, still they did not have the navigational skills needed to bring them back home again. Voyages into strange seas must have been one-way voyages into exile.

Supporting the accidental voyaging hypothesis are interviews by sea captains with Pacific islanders found adrift in canoes. Caught in storms, and driven by forces adverse to their own safety and well-being, often these drifters were completely at the mercy of wind and wave, fortunate to be found and to be rendered aid. Many had no idea where they were, no idea of the direction to their home island. And even if they did, still they had little chance of making it back home in canoes of little windward capability.

Adding weight to the hypothesis was the 1947 *Kon Tiki* expedition. Exciting in concept, this brave venture demonstrated that it is possible for a balsa-log raft to drift from South America into Polynesia. Sails were hoisted to hasten the craft's speed through the water. Still it was a drift voyage, a downwind, one-way journey toward a destination unknown. A raft running on wind and wave has no windward capability, no way of getting back home. Drifting is passive and landfall a fortuitous event.

Forty thousand years ago, according to the intentional voyaging hypothesis, the remote ancestors of the people of Oceania were living at the Pacific edge of Asia. Poised and ready for penetration into the Pacific, they had not yet the capability of sailing eastward into wind and wave.

The earth was colder than it is now. Great ice caps covered polar regions and extended as continental glaciers as far south as the Ohio River valley. Islands were larger and their shores closer to each other, with sea level lower by 250 feet than it is today. A person might then have walked from New Guinea to Australia and on to Tasmania.

A warming period followed. Ice melted, glaciers retreated, and the seas began rising. Not only did islands diminish in size in the encroaching sea, the distances between their shores increased. Human dwellers on Asia's shores had by then found ways of making tools and fashioning canoes so that they could sail beyond the horizon to islands they knew to be out there.

But how would they know? Messages are coming all the time from other islands, messages wafted on the wind, carried in the cloud, and on the surface of the sea.

It may be that the stars suggested it. Since the brightest star in the sky travels directly over Tahiti, perhaps other bright stars mark important islands: "What islands must there be lying beneath the path of that brilliant star to the north, Hōkūle'a [Arcturus]?"

Also suggesting the possibility of land to the north would be the flight of birds, migratory birds such as the golden plover. The plover is one of four types of shore birds (the others are the ruddy turnstone, the sanderling, and the wandering tattler) that fly from Siberia or Alaska to winter in Hawai'i.

Studies reported by the Audubon Society suggest that some of these birds actually overfly Hawai'i and go directly to the Marquesas or Tuamotus. A wonderful mechanism there is in the brain of the migratory bird for finding islands—always the same islands, the same place on that island. Each year you welcome back the one you know, perhaps the one with the broken leg. You see it hopping around awkwardly each winter until, of course, the year comes when you see it no more.

For centuries the people of old had been moving eastward out of Asia into the wind and wave, island-hopping toward new lands in the direction of the rising sun. What a remarkable leap of faith it must have been, as well as a new mode of thinking, to go looking for land to the north in that lonely and empty sea!

Lonely and empty it is indeed. Hawai'i in its natural state is perhaps the most isolated place on this planet. No land is there to the east for 2,400 miles. Land to the west lies twice that distance, except for tiny Wake Island and a cluster of coral atolls at the north end of the Marianas.

Three thousand years ago Polynesians were living in Samoa and Tonga. A thousand years later they had reached Tahiti, the Tubuai-Austral Islands, the Tuamotus, and the Marquesas. And a thousand years ago the settling of Polynesia was complete.

Chant, legend, song, dance, and story tell of repeated voyaging between Hawai'i and "Tahiti of the Golden Haze." Drift voyaging cannot account for that extensive contact, since wind and wave move parallel to the equator, not across it: drift is simply not possible. That impossibility has been confirmed by a computer simulation model for the settling of Polynesia. Some form of locomotion, a sail or paddle, is needed in such purposeful voyaging.

For years the controversy over the settling of Polynesia continued. Each side added evidence to support its own view. Here, though, the argument rested. Deadlocked. Not from a shortage of opinion but from a shortage of data. For no one really knew the capabilities of the voyaging canoe since none had sailed in centuries. Nor had the art of wayfinding been demonstrated over the long Tahiti-Hawai'i route in recent times. All that could be said had been said. Only the appearance of new data could break the impasse.

NEW WAYS TO OLD WAYS IN POLYNESIA

The Polynesian Voyaging Society (PVS) was organized to provide data to add to our knowledge. Taking the point of view that intentional voyaging best accounts for the known patterns of settlement within Polynesia, PVS cofounders Ben Finney, Tommy Holmes, and Herb Kane came up with an idea both brilliant and simple: create a vessel similar to the ancient Polynesian voyaging canoe and sail it to Tahiti and back in the ancient manner—without navigational instruments.

Replicating an artifact and sailing it in search of the mind of ancient people is a venture in "experimental archaeology." A modern vessel, though, can in no way be an ancient one. Materials are no longer the same. Trees of suitable length for hollowing out into hulls no longer grow in the forests. Nor are there navigators living in Hawai'i who, having apprenticed themselves to wayfinding at the age of six, are masters of the art a dozen years later, then capable of guiding a canoe to distant lands.

The canoe built by the Polynesian Voyaging Society is a fusion of ancient design and modern shipbuilding skills. Its two 60-foot hulls are made of plywood, fiberglassed, and bridged with ten crossbeams of laminated oak. The hulls are lashed to the crossbeams with 5 miles of dacron line, the canoe is fitted with sails of modern synthetic materials, and it has watertight compartments. All of this, of course, for good reason. For when you are building a vessel that hasn't been made in centuries, there's simply a lot you don't know. So it's a good idea to stick with your own technology and build into the canoe the strength you are used to.

Compromises and concessions had to be made. One principle, though, was rigidly adhered to, guiding decisions all the way along in the building of this craft—*performance accuracy.* For this to be a valid scientific experiment, the canoe must perform much in the manner of the ancient canoe. Modern modifications in hull design, such as shaping a small keel on the bottom of the canoe for better windward capability, could not be allowed; nor were deviations from traditional lashing forms acceptable.

The canoe was completed on the sand beach of Kualoa on the windward side of the island of O'ahu and launched in March of 1975. So sacred a place was Kualoa in ancient times that sails of passing canoes dipped in recognition of its *mana*. A fitting place for the launching.

A conch shell sounded and the crew gathered beside the canoe. Ka'upena Wong, attired in ceremonial white, chanted a blessing and named the canoe after the bright star Hōkūleʻa, "star of happiness," that passes directly over Hawaiʻi.

"E hoʻomākaukau!"

Scores of persons made ready by picking up the lines.

"E alu like!"

All pulled together and *Hōkūleʻa* sprang to life. Speeding down the sand, covered with palm fronds, it skimmed lightly onto the sea. And, to the measured rhythm of chant, was heard—for the first time in centuries—the sound of paddles slapping against the sides of a voyaging canoe.

Tahiti, 1976

Hōkūleʻa was outfitted; extensive sea trials followed, and with each trial it was found that changes were needed. Gunwales were raised and sails were modified from their original petroglyph design. It was a time for learning, a time for finding out how to make the parts work together as a whole.

Hōkūleʻa proved to be a sea-kindly craft as it traveled among the islands of Hawaiʻi. A return trip from Kauaʻi, though, was nearly its undoing. For in the Kauaʻi Channel, with a crew inexperienced in handling the canoe, it encountered a sea that flooded the starboard hull, causing it to founder.

Help was needed. Tommy Holmes put his surfboard in the water and paddled some 9 miles to the island of Kauaʻi to summon aid. Meanwhile, the Seaflite hydrofoil *Kamehameha* came to the aid of the stricken vessel. Ironically, it was this same channel that had twice defeated King Kamehameha two centuries earlier in his attempt to unite the islands under his rule.

It was a dark day for the Polynesian Voyaging Society. Would *Hōkūleʻa* ever sail again? Many had serious doubts. However, the concept of rediscovering Hawaiʻi's sailing heritage was so compelling and community support for the idea so warm that repairs were made and soon the canoe was back at sea, ready to set out for Tahiti.

Two questions were addressed on that 1976 voyage:

- Is it possible for a modern version of an ancient Polynesian voyaging canoe to reach Tahiti from Hawaiʻi?
- Can human navigation, as expressed in the wayfinding art, assure successful landfall?

Chief navigator for that voyage would be Mau Piailug, a master wayfinder from the island of Satawal in the Central Carolines of

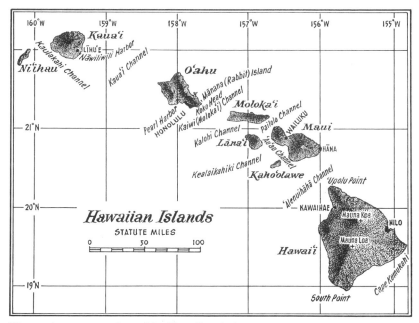

The southeastern portion of the Hawaiian chain

Micronesia. Documenting his work would be David Lewis, famous for his investigations in non-instrument navigation. Responsible for guiding *Hōkūleʻa* through the treacherous atoll waters of the Tuamotu Islands would be Rodo Williams.

The three met with astronomer George Bunton and navigator Louis Valier in the Bishop Museum Planetarium to search the simulated sky for navigational clues. Never before had Mau been south of the equator where the North Star, which he relies upon so much in his navigation, could not be seen. "We try," he said. Evidently the principles of Carolinian navigation he knows so well are generalizable to a long Hawaiʻi-Tahiti route of great latitude change.

Hōkūleʻa left Honolulu in late April of 1976 for a week's preparation at Honolua Bay, nestled in the white cliffs at the northern tip of the island of Maui. Elaborate ritual preceded the Maui departure. Unity was expressed in *ʻohana,* the concept of family, and in *hoʻoponopono,* an ancient form of problem solving. The rights, honors, privileges, and responsibilities of passage were ceremonially conferred. Then Mau spoke to the crew.

"Your captain is your mother and your father. He will tell you when to eat and when to sleep. Listen to him. Make happy. And we will all see the land we are going to."

A final blessing, the singing of "Hawai'i Aloha," and on May 1, 1976, for the first time in centuries a double-hulled voyaging canoe left Hawai'i bound for Tahiti.

Outriggers escorted *Hōkūle'a* out of Honolua Bay and into the open sea. For the next five days the canoe, captained by Kawika Kapahulehua, struggled into strong trade winds to clear Cape Kumukahi, the easternmost point in the Hawaiian Islands.

Mau Piailug, navigating from the stern of the windward hull, scarcely moved from that place during the month it took to complete the voyage. For four weeks he concentrated on his task, seeing, sensing, and knowing his way to Tahiti.

On its 31st day at sea, *Hōkūle'a* made landfall at the island of Mataiva, the westernmost atoll in the Tuamotu group. Two days later it sailed into Pape'ete Harbor for a tumultuous welcome by perhaps the largest gathering of Polynesians in modern times. The concept of the canoe as a means for rediscovering ancient ties so profoundly affected the Tahitians that some day they too will build a canoe and sail it in search of their own seafaring past.

The 1976 voyage of *Hōkūle'a* showed that it is possible for a modern double-hulled canoe of ancient design to reach Tahiti from Hawai'i. Also, that human navigation can assure continuous orientation to an island destination. An account of the building of the canoe and the events of 1976 is given in Ben Finney's book *Hokule'a: The Way to Tahiti*.

Mau returned to Satawal. "With him went our knowledge of the wayfinding art," says Nainoa Thompson. "We had not yet learned enough from him to make the voyage on our own. We would have to continue learning and exploring."

Since Mau was not aboard on the return voyage, instrument navigators guided *Hōkūle'a* back to Hawai'i. Even so, for Nainoa the return voyage was a time of learning. One night while the canoe was still near Tahiti, he watched two bright stars slowly descending the western sky. Just above the horizon they seemed to pause, then wink out as they set simultaneously. Nainoa's imagination was ignited by the event for he knew that this simultaneity would change as

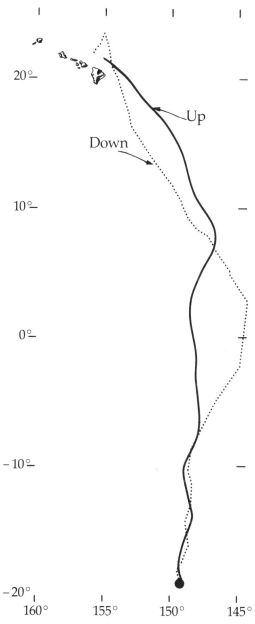

The 1976 voyages of *Hōkūleʻa:* "down" and "up"
courses compared

the canoe moved northward. In a flash of insight—insight favoring the prepared mind—he knew that here was a smaller part of a larger entity, a way for finding out where in the world he was. Later he came to the planetarium and developed the concept of synchronous rising and setting star pairs for latitude determination.

Because Nainoa's mind was so open to new experiences he would have many such shocks of recognition along his path of learning. Another shock was that of knowing without seeing:

Back before the 1976 trip we were working on the canoe lashings. One evening after work we were sitting around talking story. Mau Piailug was with us. I didn't really know him then. But he talked about the Southern Cross and how important it was to him in his navigation. I didn't know the sky at that time; in fact, I hardly knew the Southern Cross. He described it, though, and said that it was standing on the horizon right outside the *hale*. We went out and looked. There it was, right where he said it would be! It blew my mind that he could know where it was without even seeing it.

Kealaikahiki

*T*he 1976 voyage had shown that gaining initial "easting" by sailing to the northeast out of Maui and into the northeast trade winds is an arduous task. Volleys of sea spray continually drench the crew as the canoe meets the swells nearly head-on. It's a cold, wet, and windy beginning for a month-long ocean voyage.

Is it possible that the channel called Kealaikahiki, as the name suggests, might have served ancient navigators as the "path to Tahiti?"

A study of remnants of oral tradition led Gordon Pi'ianai'a, chief motivator of the Kealaikahiki project, to believe so—that the leeward, rather than the windward side of the island chain would have been a more likely starting route for the ancients. It would offer a gentle beginning for a long journey and the required easting could be gained gradually rather than abruptly.

The Polynesian Voyaging Society put the idea to a test. *Hōkūle'a* sailed out of Honolulu on April 1, 1977, pausing at Mānele Bay on the island of Lāna'i to await a favorable wind. On the morning of the fourth, a brisk wind was blowing out of the north—an ideal wind for the Kealaikahiki venture. The north wind comes only occasionally. It is a transition wind, following a low pressure system moving through the islands and ceasing with the return of the trades.

Hōkūle'a sped across the 16-mile Kealaikahiki Channel in less than three hours to reach the lee side of the island of Kaho'olawe just before noon. Here the canoe was virtually becalmed as it moved slowly along high sea cliffs. By late afternoon, though, it had moved into strong winds blowing through 'Alenuihāhā Channel, and at sunset was 40 miles west of 'Upolu Point on the island of Hawai'i.

Jupiter glowed intensely above the setting sun. One by one the

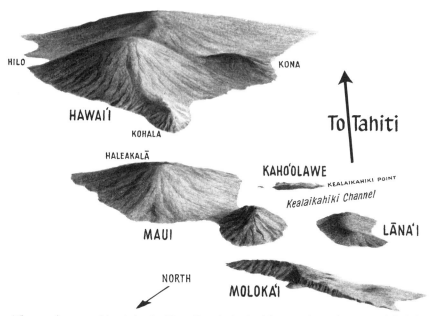

HILO

KONA

HAWAIʻI

KOHALA

HALEAKALĀ

KAHOʻOLAWE

KEALAIKAHIKI POINT

Kealaikahiki Channel

To Tahiti

MAUI

LĀNAʻI

NORTH

MOLOKAʻI

The southeastern islands in the Hawaiian chain, looking southward over Kealaikahiki Point toward Tahiti

stars appeared in the evening twilight and soon the waxing gibbous moon would be rising. While the horizon was still visible the instrument navigators aboard, using sextant, chronometer, and star tables, began working out the canoe's position.

Without knowledge of what the instrument navigators were determining, Nainoa checked the course of *Hōkūleʻa* against the background of steering stars. Then he set a course slightly east of south to avoid yet another wind shadow, that of the island of Hawaiʻi.

All night long Nainoa watched the sky and sea, checking the relationship of the canoe's direction relative to the stars and its path through the water so that he could determine its apparent course. The true course would later be plotted from the navigational fixes; the two compared would be an essential part of the research.

"The wind is pushing us south at a speed that is hard for me to determine," reasoned Nainoa. "Morning will probably find us west of Mauna Loa, and I think we'll see the sun coming up from behind the big volcano."

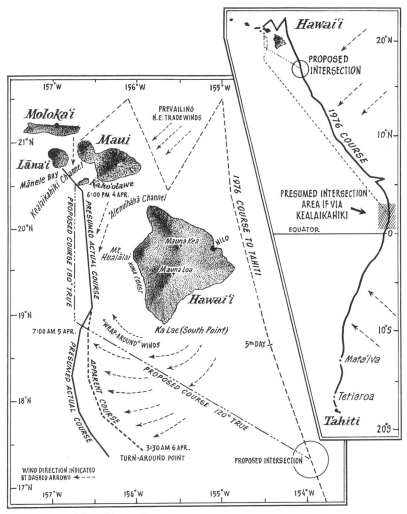

The 1977 Kealaikahiki experiment

A 15-knot variable headwind sprang up from the southeast at three in the morning. Southeast? A headwind? The prevailing trade winds are from the northeast, not southeast. Could this be a "wrap-around" wind, swinging in a curve around the southern end of the island of Hawai'i? At any rate it was forcing *Hōkūle'a* uncontrollably on a course west of south.

Stars faded and disappeared in the morning twilight. Soon the sun would be rising. All crew members searched the horizon for land. Clouds added to the problem of seeing. Suddenly the sky brightened as the rim of the sun appeared over an empty sea.

No land. No land anywhere.

"We must have been making better headway than my estimate had allowed," reasoned Nainoa. "My guess is that we're south of Hawai'i and these are the wrap-around winds. Now we must turn east and hold that course as best we can."

All day *Hōkūle'a* rode up and down large swells coming from the northeast. At times the sun was visible, allowing the instrument navigators a morning line of position that they followed up with a noontime fix. Winds were becoming more northerly in the afternoon, so Nainoa ordered a course turned even higher into the wind. Cloudiness increased, and at sunset the sky became so overcast that the instrument navigators were unable to determine the canoe's position.

The canoe moved eastward into a cloudy night. Fortunately the cloudiness began breaking up, revealing at midnight the Southern Cross standing upright on the southern horizon. For the past several hours the canoe had been holding a steady course to the southeast. When it seemed certain that it could continue holding the course, a decision was made to terminate the experiment. Under a cloudless, starry sky, *Hōkūle'a* came about and headed back to Kona.

And what of the results of this experiment? A projection of the course that *Hōkūle'a* had been holding for several hours prior to turn-around shows it intersecting the 1976 course line slightly north of the equator. A line projected, though, is not necessarily a course sailed, for the sailor is bound to the wind. Given the same conditions, we can predict a Tuamotu landfall. Conditions, though, are never the same.

From this experiment, we know that Kealaikahiki offers a smooth beginning for a long journey—smoother than the windward departure. It is a logical departure point and, as such, must certainly be in line with tradition.

Kealaikahiki *is* a way to Tahiti.

Wait for a north wind. Or accept Gordon Pi'ianai'a's advice and "be prepared to tack."

High Wind, High Hope

*I*t was right after the Kealaikahiki project that Nainoa began working in the planetarium. Two or three times a week he would appear, often with his fishing partner, Bruce Blankenfeld, and two hours of work would begin.

"Canopus at the meridian," says Nainoa. The machine whirs and stars rush across the sky as I bring the second brightest star in the sky to the meridian.

"Now slow . . . ." Nainoa and Bruce team up to collect data, one watching the eastern horizon and the other the western for the rising and setting of bright stars. We move through the first night in ten minutes, each of them calling out the moment an important star rises or sets.

Antares appears on the eastern horizon and Nainoa says, "Okay. Sun's coming up." While I move the sun rapidly across the sky so that another night can begin, Nainoa writes in his notebook:

At 20° north [the latitude of Hawai'i], Gienah rises as the tail of Canis Major reaches the meridian. Avior is almost at the meridian when Spica and Hōkūle'a are rising. With Regulus at the meridian, the False Cross and Southern Cross are tilted at the same angle.

This is how it begins. Four full pages of such entries follow with data he collected in many sessions, just for the latitude of 20° N.

"Okay, now the equator."

The angle of the machine with respect to the horizon decreases. Polaris touches the northern horizon, and in the opposite direction the Southern Cross rises to prominence. Here at 0° latitude we go through several equatorial nights:

Navi sets as Megrez rises. With Sirius at the meridian, Procyon and Betelgeuse are equal distances from the meridian. Achernar sets as the False Cross rises on its side. When Avior is on the meridian Alkaid is 3° above the horizon.

Several more pages of such entries follow for just the equator. Gathering data is tedious but a necessary first step. From particulars, patterns emerge. And in greater coherencies would be the knowledge he would rely upon in maintaining orientation in fifty-six days and nights at sea.

"Okay, now back to 20° N."

He's following out a hunch? Maybe. Checking something out? Perhaps. A moment of insight? I hope so. I wait. It's quiet here in the darkness. I could be doing something else. My mind is wandering.

But his mind leaps to a new connectedness. He's relating something at 0° to what he saw at 20°. Could be. I really don't know how his mind works. Nor my own. I'm speculating, trying to stay interested when I don't know what's going on. I could ask.

Puzzlement? The cognitive leap? A broader base of understanding from which new knowledge will come? Or maybe it's time to go home. I mentally shake myself and recall Jerome Bruner's statement, "It is difficult to catch and record, no less to understand, the swift flight of man's mind operating at its best."

"Okay, now Tahiti." The machine bends farther downward and looks like a long-legged, large-headed antidiluvian bird of some sort.

When Avior is at the meridian and Dubhe is setting you are 16° south. At Tahiti, Alioth is as high above the horizon as it is beneath Cor Caroli.

Nainoa's head was filled with detail. So, too, his three-ring, yellow-covered notebook with divider sections labeled:

> Night direction-keeping using moon and planets
> Day direction-keeping using sun, moon, and ocean
> Zenith stars
> North Star
> Synchronous pairs
> Expanded landfall
> Birds
> Clouds
> Phosphorescense
> Drift objects
> Coloration of water

Eventually he would compress the data into rules of thumb, and then become free of the notebook.

"We'll sail to Tahiti on the first good wind after March 15th," said Captain Dave Lyman in a newspaper interview. The announcement was no surprise; it served to heighten community interest, as it also increased crew anxiety. Nainoa redoubled his effort:

At 20° north, Avior is at the meridian when Shedar is setting and Hōkū-le'a rising. At 8° or 9° north Avior is at the meridian as Kochab rises. At the equator Alkaid rises when Avior is at the meridian.

"Our main purpose," said Ben Young, head of the steering committee, "is to document non-instrument navigation. We will also test the *lauhala* sails and do some food experiments and preservation tests. *Hōkūle'a* is in good shape."

Hōkūleʻa crew members and Bishop Museum personnel at a training session in the planetarium, February 1978. From left: Mike Tongg, president of PVS; Dr. Ben Young, chairman of the steering committee; Buddy McGuire; Jerry Muller; Kikila Hugho; Will Kyselka; Marion Lyman; Steve Somsen; Kip Kauka; Nainoa Thompson; Dr. Kenneth P. Emory, chairman of anthropology; Dr. Edward Creutz, director of the Bishop Museum

Hōkūleʻa was provisioned and ready to go in mid-March. A long *ʻawa* ceremony preceded departure. Each crew member drank from the ceremonial bowl, an act symbolically separating those committed to the sea from those remaining on the land. Afterward, as I talked with Nainoa I felt the separation complete.

A *lauhala* sail, soft and golden and of the type woven in Kapingamarangi, was hoisted. Kenneth Emory, dean of Pacific anthropology and author of the classic monograph on Kapingamarangi, was delighted. "This is the first time I've seen it." It would be the last time, too, for soon the sail would be shredded by powerful winds.

Standing beside him, his wife Marguerite told of her experiences in Tahiti when as a child she had so often watched canoes departing for other islands. She dipped and swayed in spontaneous hula as her hands told the story of canoes moving out onto the sea at twilight, their sails decreasing in size with increasing distance, then being engulfed in the darkness where navigators would turn to the stars for direction.

The sun was setting and the First Quarter Moon was high in the southern sky. We sang "Aloha 'Oe," and the canoe moved away from its mooring. Outriggers escorted it out of Ala Wai Channel and into the twilight. Wind caught the canoe's sails and carried it gracefully toward Diamond Head. A jubilant shout rang out from the canoe, "See you in Tahiti!"

Driven by strong winds from the northeast, *Hōkūle'a* moved swiftly into the Moloka'i Channel. Swells were high, but the canoe had ridden out such seas before. However, this time it was heavily laden with food and supplies for a month's journey. The added weight put unusual stress on the canoe, making it difficult to handle. Turning off-wind eased the strain but it also caused the sea to wash in over the gunwales, filling the starboard compartments and depressing the lee hull. Winds pushing on the sails rotated the lighter windward hull around the submerged lee hull, now dead in the water. Five hours after leaving Ala Wai Harbor, *Hōkūle'a* was upside-down in the sea between O'ahu and Moloka'i.

All that night fourteen persons clung to the hulls of the stricken vessel, huddling to protect themselves as best they could from wind and wave. Daylight came. Airplanes flew overhead but no one saw *Hōkūle'a*. Adding to the problems of the crew was exposure to the sun, intense and nearly overhead at mid-day. Most alarming, though, was the fact that the canoe was drifting away from airline routes, decreasing its chance of being spotted.

Snake Ah Hee left on a surfboard to summon aid. When a low-flying airplane appeared, he assumed that the overturned canoe had been seen, and he returned. After a long period of waiting it became clear that it was not so.

Eddie Aikau wanted to go for help. An expert waterman, he had saved the lives of many swimmers in trouble in the powerful surf of Waimea Bay on the north shore of O'ahu. Nainoa paddled out with him a short distance to test the surfboard and waves. Eddie would go alone. The crew, clinging to the overturned hulls, watching in silence as he rode the waves into a fate not unknown to many of the people of old who sailed toward distant lands.

For days, planes and boats searched the channel for Eddie. The initial hope of finding him gradually gave way to the pain and agony of a reality that had once seemed an impossibility.

Waimea Bay

Six weeks later dozens of outrigger canoes lined the sandy beach of Waimea Bay, the Reverend Abraham Akaka of Kawaiaha'o Church expressing the feeling of the community in a final tribute to Eddie's way of helping others. A prayer was given, a song was sung; then Eddie's friends paddled out onto the bay to cover its surface with flower leis.

A journey that began in high wind and high hope was completed at Waimea Bay.

PRELUDE TO 1980

Nainoa went to the island of Hawai'i to sail alone out onto the sea, dealing with his grief in a solitary way as men often do. A few months later he was back in the planetarium studying the stars. Even though there seemed not a vestige of hope ever again of sailing *Hōkūle'a* to Tahiti, still for some reason Nainoa had to continue increasing his knowledge of navigation.

Along with his renewed interest in his heritage came an important event that made ancient ways even more comprehensible. Puaniho appeared, and with his presence our whole concept of Polynesian sailing expanded.

Puaniho Tauotaha lives in Tautira, a village on the southeastern end of Tahiti. He came to Hawai'i to build *koa* canoes. One day we went with him into the mountains to watch this master craftsman practice his art. Here in a grove of *koa* trees on windward O'ahu he prepared to cut a tree to make a canoe. We stood quiet in this quiet place, with the 2,000-foot fluted columns of the windward Pali behind us.

In ancient times, each step in the building of the voyaging canoe was attended to with appropriate ceremony; the product of the effect would be a way of moving powerfully over the sea, a way of realizing the hopes and dreams of a people as expressed in song and dance.

But neither rite nor ritual accompanies the cutting of this tree. Instead, casualness pervades. If ceremony exists it must be internal. While Puaniho sharpens each tooth on his chain saw, crew candidate Louie Chung whistles and sings in the forest. The sharpening completed, Puaniho pulls the starter cord and the saw roars into action. He watches it rotating slowly on the ground, listening for nuances of imperfection which he must correct. Man and machine tune up for a task.

The saw snarls, the tree falls, and all is silent again. Puaniho trims the branches and he walks back and forth on the trunk, feeling its twist with his bare feet. He says nothing, then hunkers down to study the 50-foot log. His wife, Mahine, smiles and serves us food.

Puaniho's task for the day is that of carving away the parts of the tree so that the canoe can emerge. A stretched string gives him a line to follow. With a chain saw almost as tall as he, he follows that line and the wood chips fly. How effortlessly, how artfully he uses the saw!

The saw in his hand is an integral part of him, not an external object. It's the way his mind shapes an idea. Everything is done by eye. No measurement. Each canoe is unique. Measurement is needed only where parts are interchangeable. After two hours of

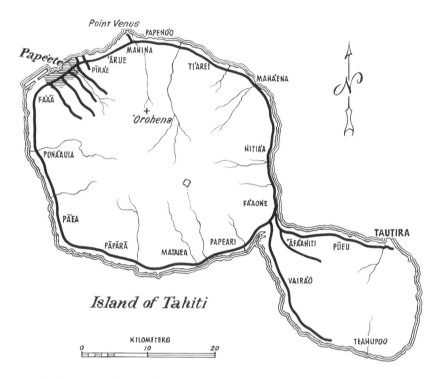

Island of Tahiti

work the canoe is roughed out and ready to be taken to a canoe shed for a long, slow curing.

While in Hawai'i, Puaniho built several canoes. Then he and his wife went back to Tahiti. His skill had shown how quickly a tree in the forest can become a way for reaching distant islands.

Nainoa returned to his work at the planetarium. Although the planetarium instrument presents the southern sky remarkably well, it is not the real sky. He must go into the Southern Hemisphere to know those stars personally. And while in Tahiti he would stay with Puaniho's family in the canoe-building village of Tautira.

Nights are dark in Tautira. Nainoa went to study the stars, but it rained—for the first nine nights. The rain, however, turned out to be a blessing in disguise, for though it hid the stars it opened up new ideas. During that time the winds came from the west, from the direction the first explorers had come from. He could see, as he could have seen in no other way, how the Polynesians might have used such winds in moving eastward from Tonga and Samoa to the Cooks and Tahiti.

Eventually the clouds moved on and stars shone down on Tautira. Observing those stars, however, was not an entirely happy occasion for Nainoa. "I was confused. Nothing was right. I couldn't find the star patterns I was used to. I felt sad because all that work we did in the planetarium seemed to be of no use here."

Next night the sky was clear. So, too, was Nainoa's perception of it. He had by then adjusted to that nearly 40° latitude change and no longer was the sky a stranger to him. What was in his mind was also far above his head, that happy, starry night in Tautira.

Stellar Clues

*N*ainoa returned to the planetarium, knowing that he must learn more and eventually sail that Hawai'i-Tahiti route. Canoe, sea, and stars—the concept was clearer to him, and the Polynesian Voyaging Society itself was committed to another voyage.

But how would he learn?

His was a lonely task, for traditional ways of learning were no longer open to him. He had no ancient navigational chant to go on, no master to learn from, no peers to talk with. Nor was he immersed in a culture in which the wayfinding art is deeply embedded.

The last Polynesian to sail in the old way was Tevake, a navigator from the Polynesian outlier island of Santa Cruz. When in 1970 Tevake knew his personal existence was nearing an end, he held a celebration in the nature of a formal farewell. Then, in the manner of his people, he sailed alone out onto the sea on a voyage of no return.

The art and the last artist of Polynesian navigation vanished on that voyage. With Tevake's passing, Polynesians were left with only the memories of their wayfinding past, with fragments of chant and legend and epic accounts of navigators who sailed the sea in search of distant lands.

For Nainoa the next two years would be a time for learning, a time for exploring the heavens in a manner not available to the ancients. He would continue gathering data, searching for patterns, transforming information into knowledge, and putting it all into comprehensible form.

A feeling for geometric relationship guided his exploration. Fundamental in his star knowledge was the concept of a "celestial sphere."

THE CELESTIAL SPHERE

Stars are bright points of light on a dark background. They appear as if stuck onto the "dome of night," the celestial sphere. Actually they are not fixed to anything. In fact they are quite independent, each moving in its own direction at speeds measured in tens of kilometers per second. In spite of the celestial rush, stars are all so far away that we see no change at all in the heavens in so short a span as a human lifetime.

Nainoa found useful the great circles on the celestial sphere: equator, meridian, and ecliptic. The celestial equator is the earth's equator projected onto the celestial sphere. The meridian is the great circle that runs from north to south and through the point overhead. And the ecliptic is the sun's annual path among the stars.

The ecliptic is tilted 23.5° from the celestial equator. Moon and planets never stray far from this line—the earth-sun plane. A dozen constellations lie along the ecliptic. Each, except one, is seen as an animal form. During the year the sun spends a month in each of these star groups—in the "circle of animals," the zodiac.

Nainoa developed four ways for determining direction, six for determining latitude.

DETERMINING DIRECTION

The canoe on the open ocean is at the center of a circle, the edge of which is three, perhaps four miles distant. Beyond that horizon—5 billion times farther—is the nearest of our navigational stars, Alpha Centauri. The circle and the stars form the "star compass."

Star Compass

A star compass surrounds the sailor at sea. Stars rise at particular points in the east and set at corresponding points in the west. The rising or setting point of a star, measured clockwise along the horizon from north and expressed in degrees, is its azimuth.

Stars trace arcs of circles on the celestial sphere as the earth turns. Near the equator, where they pass across the sky most rapidly, the arcs are longest. But in polar regions, where they move slower, the arcs are shorter. Some stars near the celestial poles neither rise nor set; they are circumpolar.

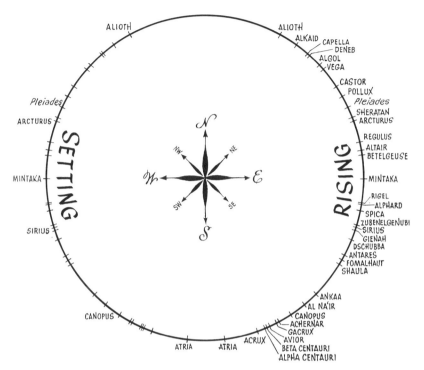

Nainoa's star compass

Nainoa used thirty-six stars to give seventy-two points on his star compass. He considered the sun as a special star (which it certainly is to us) that can be used in keeping direction, one that shifts its azimuth according to season. Planets are always near the ecliptic and may be useful on voyages of short duration.

The experienced navigator needs only one clue, only one star on a cloudy night, to orient the whole star compass with respect to the canoe.

The azimuth of a star changes as the observer changes latitude. The shift is greatest for those closest to the poles, smallest for those nearest the equator.

Star Culmination

A rising star continues climbing into the sky until it reaches the meridian—its culmination—then begins descending. A point directly beneath a culminating star is either true north or south.

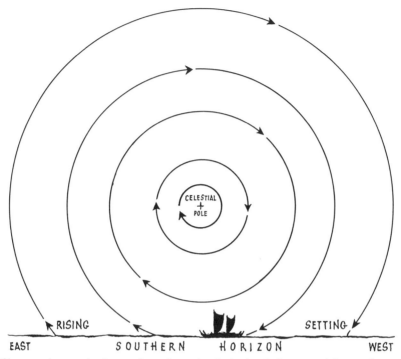

Circumpolar stars in the southern sky make clockwise circles around the south celestial pole

The North Star, though, is a special case. It is in continuous culmination. At least that is true in our era. Actually, it makes a tiny circle on the celestial sphere, a circle that will grow in size over the next 13,000 years due to "earth wobbling" (precession). During our lifetime the point beneath Polaris is due north.

Star Pairs

Nainoa found it easier to work with pairs of stars rather than single stars. A line through a meridional pair (two stars of the same celestial longitude) is a north-south line. The stars at the top and bottom of the Southern Cross, for instance, are of the same celestial longitude. So when Crux is standing straight up, south is at the horizon below it.

But Crux doesn't have to be standing at the horizon to be useful.

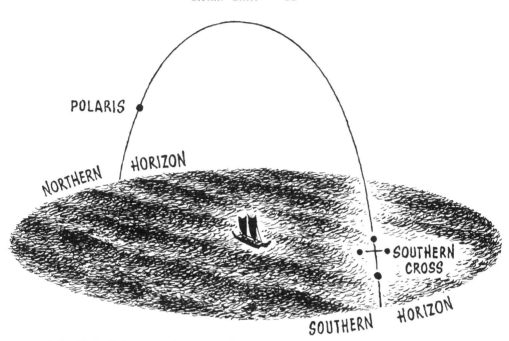

A double-hulled canoe at the center of the circle of sea and sky, moving in the direction of the Southern Cross

Even when it's rising, tilted on its side, a line through the staff still points to the south celestial pole which, for the observer in Hawai'i, is 19° below the horizon.

The two brightest stars in the sky, Sirius and Canopus, form a prominent meridional pair. Since Sirius lags Canopus by 20 minutes, Nainoa prefers the fainter star, Mirzam, to pair with Canopus and form a more precise pair with less than 2 minutes separating their individual meridional arrivals. Nainoa uses eighteen meridional star pairs for direction keeping.

The "Cut of the Moon"

Still another clue to direction is the moon, particularly when it is a crescent. A line through the moon's "terminator" (the line dividing day and night on the lunar surface) is at certain times a north-south line. Nainoa calls it "the cut of the moon."

That happens when both sun and moon are on the celestial equator. However, since the sun during the year wanders 23.5° north and south of the equator (and the moon an additional 5° as it circles the earth twelve times), the "cut of the moon" as a direction-keeping device becomes increasingly complex.

It works, but it is cumbersome, requiring the navigator to keep in mind the continually changing relationship of sun and moon. Without that knowledge the "cut of the moon" is only an approximation to be used when other clues are not available.

DETERMINING LATITUDE

We have looked at four ways that Nainoa developed for determining direction. He also worked out six ways of using the stars for determining latitude.

Zenith Star

The simplest (and least precise) way for determining latitude is from the zenith star, the star that passes directly overhead. Look straight up. If Sirius is above, you're at the latitude of Tahiti; if Arcturus, your latitude is that of Hawai'i.

The lack of precision in this method is simply the difficulty in finding the point overhead. Again look straight up and this time pick a point you think to be the zenith. Turn around, face the opposite direction and try it again. Chances are this time you'll pick a point several degrees from your first one.

Finding the zenith is hard enough to do on dry land but for the sailor at sea it is a confusion compounded. So difficult is determining the zenith that modern instrument navigators measure the distance from the horizon to the star and subtract from 90°.

Nainoa found the zenith star method of no use at all. Perhaps the zenith star concept is of greater apocryphal value than of any practical utility, a way of identifying an island by saying something such as, "My island lies beneath the path of Hōkūle'a."

Height of Polaris

Polaris is almost, not quite, directly over the earth's north rotational pole. It's at your zenith if you're standing at the North Pole but at

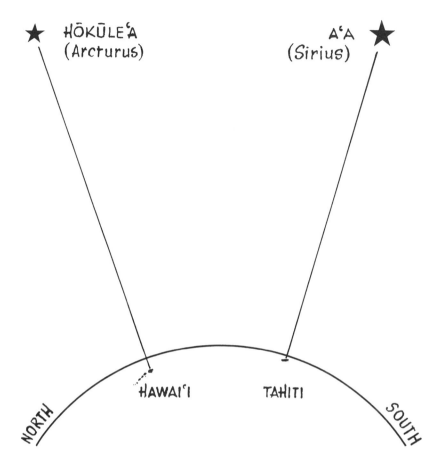

Hōkūle'a is the zenith star for Hawai'i; Sirius, the zenith star for Tahiti

the horizon if you're on the equator. The observer at 20° N sees it 20° above the horizon. In other words, the elevation of the North Star corresponds to the observer's latitude.

Polaris is a problem for Nainoa—perhaps less a problem than a point of interest. Since it misses being over the earth's pole by 0.8°, it traces a circle 1.6° in diameter on the celestial sphere. It moves slightly up and down as the earth spins. When Aries is at the meridian the North Star is at its highest point above the horizon; at its lowest when Libra is at the meridian. Using only Polaris for latitude, a navigator could be off by as much as 1.6°, a hundred nautical miles. However, only a highly skilled observer could, without the use of instruments, detect so small a difference.

Star Culmination

The height of a culminating star is also a clue to latitude, provided you know how far north or south of the equator it is—its declination —and that requires measurement. Nainoa memorized the declinations of 110 stars as given in the *Index Observer's Handbook*. Canopus, for instance, lies 53° south of the celestial equator. The observer at the equator sees it culminating 37° above the southern horizon.

Meridional Star Pairs

How do you know, though, when Canopus is 37° above the horizon so that you can say you're at the equator? That's difficult. Rather than depending upon single stars, Nainoa found a pair, a proportionality, easier to read.

A good meridional pair is the staff of the Southern Cross. When the lower star (Acrux) is as high above the horizon as it is beneath the upper star (Gacrux), the observer is at 21° N, the latitude of Hawai'i. A good clue to Tahiti is the Alioth–Cor Caroli meridional pair, with Alioth as high above the horizon as it is beneath Cor Caroli.

Synchronous Star Pairs

Pairs of stars that rise (or set) simultaneously are clues to latitude. The idea occurred to Nainoa when, in returning from Tahiti aboard *Hōkūle'a* in 1976, he saw Vega and Altair rising together. Instantly he knew he had a way for determining latitude, for he knew that such simultaneity would vary with latitude change. In the planetarium he developed that idea of synchronous rising and setting pairs for latitude determination.

Synchronous setting is easier to read than rising, simply because the navigator has a long time in which to watch such a pair settling into the atmosphere. Synchronous rising, on the other hand, has no antecedents. Suddenly the pair is there, a moment hard to anticipate.

Nainoa's ways for determining direction and latitude may have ancient counterparts. We have no way of knowing, and we can only assume a convergence. His "synchronous rising and setting star pair" method may be unique. It came out of his observation of an event in nature and research at the planetarium.

Now let's see how these methods work on a simulated voyage to Tahiti.

Journey by Starlight

*F*or a better understanding of how Nainoa's navigational system works, we will take a planetarium trip from Hawai'i to Tahiti starting in mid-March. First we'll go through one night to see the changes in the sky that take place by the hour. Then we'll journey southward to see the changes that occur with a change in latitude as well as over a period of time.

The Mid-March Sky

The mid-March sun travels across the sky 2° south of the celestial equator. On the 21st of the month it crosses the equator, and at that time rises due east and sets due west. The sun at the latitude of Honolulu is in the sky exactly twelve hours, rising at 6:41 A.M., setting at 6:41 P.M. A half-hour later the brightest stars begin appearing in the twilight.

The sun itself is in the direction of Pisces the Fishes. Above the setting sun are Sheratan and Hamal, the horns of Aries the Ram. Well up in the western sky and above Orion the Giant is Taurus the Bull. The Twins, Gemini, are at the meridian and faint Cancer follows. High in the east and beneath the Big Dipper is Leo the Lion; Virgo is rising.

The star pair Mirzam and Canopus, the first of Nainoa's directional pointers, is at the meridian. Sirius follows closely. The seven brilliant stars forming the figure of Orion are shining brightly in the west.

Close to the horizon is the False Cross, an asterism, borrowing stars from two constellations, Carina the Keel, and Vela the Sail. The Keel and Sail, along with Puppis the Stern, are scattered parts of Argo Navis, the ship on which Jason and the Argonauts sailed in search of the Golden Fleece.

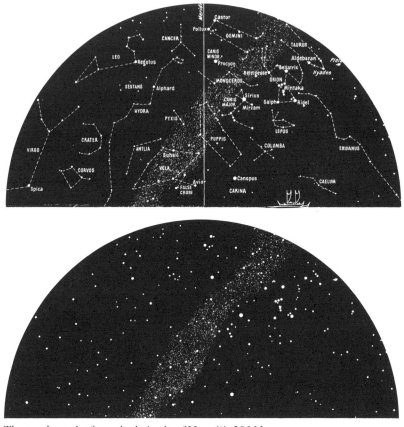

The southern sky from the latitude of Hawai'i, 20° N

Orion is divided between the two hemispheres. The "three in a row" forming his belt are known in Tonga as "the three canoe paddlers," a trio traveling right along the celestial equator. Mintaka, the westernmost star, is closest to the celestial equator, only 0.3° from it. Each lies at a moderate depth in space—1,600 light-years.

Extend a line through the "three in a row" to the southeast and you will find the brightest star, Sirius. Extend that line in the opposite direction and you'll find Aldebaran, a red-giant star marking the eye of Taurus the Bull. Beyond it to the west is the Pleiades, known also as Nā-huihui-a-Makali'i. This beautiful "cluster of little eyes" travels right over Hawai'i.

How interesting to know by what names the Polynesians of old called the stars and constellations! However, only a few such names

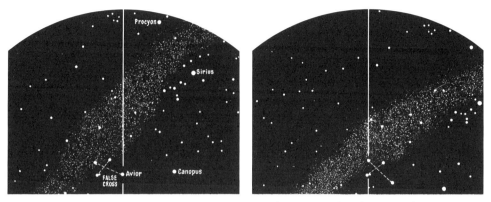

The False Cross rising, as seen from the latitude of Hawai'i. Avior, the star at the foot of the cross, reaches the meridian a half-hour before the star at the top, Kappa Velorum.

remain. When long-distance voyaging ceased centuries ago, star lore and legend useful in navigation was lost. Nainoa uses the standard Greek and Babylonian names for the constellations and Arabic names for the stars—names now officially recognized by international agreement among astronomers.

Meandering southward from the foot of Orion is the River Eridanus, the river into which Phaethon fell in his unsuccessful bid to drive the sun across the sky. The River ends with bright Achernar far to the southwest near the horizon. Mirroring that form and stretching in the opposite direction is the longest of all the constellations, Hydra the Sea Serpent.

Spica and Hōkūle'a are rising together, the first synchronous pair used for latitude determination.

Three hours after sunset Avior, the foot of the False Cross, reaches the meridian. Following it to the meridian is Kappa Velorum, the top star in the False Cross. Even though it is at the meridian, the False Cross is not yet standing upright—and will not until Crux reaches the meridian.

Rigel sets, Orion lingers, and Leo is overhead. Marking the Lion's heart is blue Regulus, 84 light-years distant. Above Leo and reaching its most favorable position for viewing at this hour is the Big Dipper.

The seven bright stars of the Big Dipper are high above us. Hawaiians called the group Nā-hiku, "the seven." A line through Merak

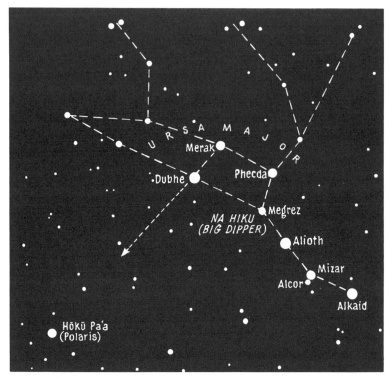

Stars in the north centering around Nā-hiku and Hōkū-paʻa

and Dubhe in the bowl of the Dipper points to Hōkū-paʻa, the "unmoving star," Polaris.

Midnight. The Southern Cross is quietly moving into the sky. An hour from now it will be standing upright at the southern horizon along with the False Cross. Shining at the top of the Southern Cross is Gacrux, a cool red-giant star 220 light-years distant. Of contrasting mode is the star at the foot of the Cross, Acrux. Bright blue in color, Acrux is a double star twice as deep into space. Nainoa uses this pair for determining direction as well as latitude. When viewed from Hawaiʻi, Acrux is 6° below Gacrux and 6° above the horizon.

A faint band of light rims the horizon at this midnight hour. Embedded in it are Scorpius, Sagittarius, and Crux. Spanning it in the northern sky is the triangle of Deneb, Vega, and Altair. The faint light is our city of stars, the Milky Way galaxy of some 200 billion stars.

Two in the morning. Alpha and Beta Centauri are parallel to the

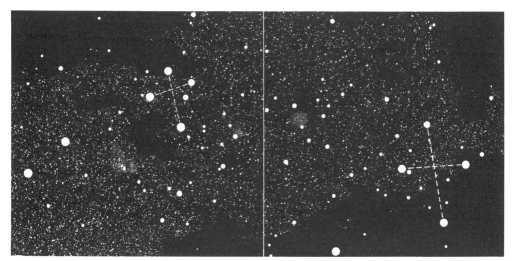

When the Southern Cross and False Cross are tilted at the same angle to the horizon, the False Cross is well beyond the meridian, shown here as a thin vertical line.

Southern Cross standing upright at the meridian

horizon, "splitting the meridian." When this pair is parallel to the horizon, the point between them is true south; at that time Hōkū-le'a is overhead.

Sweeping across the sky at three in the morning is a stellar curve uniting North Star and Southern Cross. This great curve runs from Polaris and along the curving handle of the Big Dipper to Arcturus. Then it runs to Spica and down to Crux at the southern horizon. In

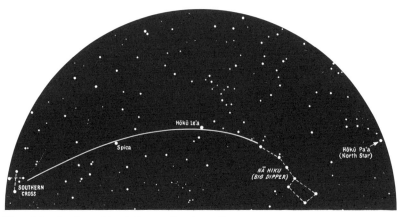

The night sky, from North Star to Southern Cross

all of Polynesia, Hawai'i is the only island chain from which both North Star and Southern Cross can be seen.

Kochab culminates and Leo sets. The Winged Horse rises as the sun comes up. One night has passed, thirty more lie ahead.

A Month to Tahiti

Two great changes take place in the sky during the month that it takes to reach Tahiti. One has to do with our traveling over the earth's surface; the other with the earth's traveling around the sun.

A change in latitude allows us to see previously unseen stars in the direction of travel. As we move south over the curve of the earth we see farther into the Southern Hemisphere and find stars not visible in Hawai'i. We also lose some northern stars.

The other change has to do with the gradual westward drift of the stars. Each night stars are slightly west of where they were the previous night. Another way of saying it is that stars rise and set four minutes earlier each night. At the end of a week, stars are in their places a half-hour earlier, and in a month they are there two hours earlier.

On our journey southward we reach a point where Canopus and Rigel set synchronously, and from Nainoa's work we know we are at a latitude of 13° N. As we continue south we will see Canopus and Mintaka set synchronously and know we're 9° N. A little farther south Canopus and Capella set together and we're at 7° N.

The trip to the equator takes two weeks. The North Star has dropped to the horizon. Stars are setting an hour earlier than they were when we began the journey. Here we're halfway between the poles of the earth where stars rise vertically and set vertically. Mintaka in Orion's belt makes the longest arc of all, for it is right on the celestial equator. It rises directly east, goes through the zenith, and sets directly west. Here at the equator we also observe something seen nowhere else on this planet: synchronously rising pairs of stars also set synchronously.

Crux moves higher into the sky as we travel into the Southern Hemisphere. We can think of it as stars increasing in height as we travel toward them. Or, as Nainoa prefers to do, we can visualize it as he expresses it, "the horizon depressing in the direction of travel."

Capella-Sirius-Pollux are synchronously setting at 13° S. A clue to the latitude of the Tuamotus is the Cor Caroli–Alioth meridional pair. Alioth is as high above the northern horizon at this latitude as it is below Cor Caroli.

In working with 110 stars, Nainoa came up with many clues to latitude. Tahiti, at 17° S, has two synchronously setting pairs— Sirius-Pollux and Mirzam-Castor. And for the navigator who looks straight up, Sirius, Gienah, Zubenelgenubi, and Sabik are zenith stars.

From Tahiti we look back into the northern sky to see the upside-down Big Dipper scraping the horizon. Arcturus is 38° lower than when we viewed it in Hawai'i. And in the southern sky, near the south celestial pole, are faint satellites of our own galaxy, the Magellanic Clouds.

Nainoa's heuristic process, his "seeking to discover," continued, and in hundreds of truly "dry runs" between Hawai'i and Tahiti, we explored the sky widely. He compacted wide ranges of information into cogent form. And he searched for connectedness that might reveal less obvious features of reality. He knew that the key to his finding islands was in knowing the bright points of light on the planetarium dome.

He collected data. Overcollected. He had to, for he was exploring new territory and had no way of knowing how much was enough or

The north celestial pole is at the center of the circle. Near it is Polaris, the end star in the handle of the Little Dipper. The Little Dipper is at this hour pouring into the Big Dipper.

The region of the sky near the south celestial pole is relatively devoid of stars. The Southern Cross, tilted slightly to the west, is at the upper center of the drawing. A line through the staff of the cross points in the direction of the south celestial pole.

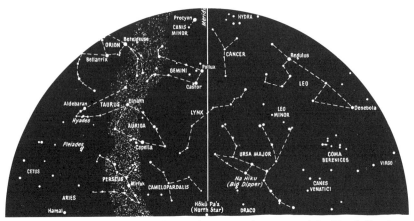

View of the northern sky as seen by an observer at the equator. The North Star is at the horizon.

what might prove to be significant. Above all, he must be competent. That takes time.

Lest our thinking become provincial, we occasionally left the tropics to venture via planetarium into polar regions. At each pole we saw Orion's belt circling the horizon. And at the north pole we watched Polaris, constant at that zenith for a six-months' night. Then during a six-months' day we watched the sun wavering up and down as it circled the horizon.

We ran time back a thousand years to see the sky as it was when Polynesians were making those early voyages between Tahiti and Hawai'i. Then back another thousand years to the time the first explorers had found Tahiti, coincident in time with the Roman conquest of Europe. Still another thousand years back to see it as the first Tongans and Samoans had seen it, a half-millennium before the Golden Age of Greece.

What a different sky 3,000 years ago! Polaris was rising and setting. The Southern Cross was traveling over Tonga. So high, in fact, was the Southern Cross that people living in Alaska would have seen it low on the southern horizon.

We wondered, in our wandering over the earth's surface and back into time, of the content of ancient navigational chants. Certainly they must have described a sky quite different from the one we know today.

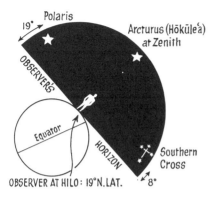

Polaris

19°

Arcturus (Hōkūle'a)
at Zenith

OBSERVER'S

Equator

HORIZON

Southern
Cross

8°

OBSERVER AT HILO: 19°N.LAT.

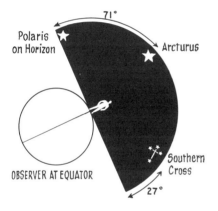

71°

Polaris
on Horizon

Arcturus

Southern
Cross

OBSERVER AT EQUATOR

27°

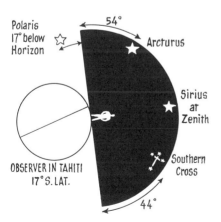

54°

Polaris
17° below
Horizon

Arcturus

Sirius
at
Zenith

Southern
Cross

OBSERVER IN TAHITI
17° S. LAT.

44°

The elevation of a star above the horizon varies as the observer changes latitude. As the observer in Hawai'i moves south, Arcturus moves out of its zenith position and closer to the northern horizon. Upon reaching Tahiti, the observer finds Sirius at the zenith.

Nainoa's mind shaped a body of knowledge and, in turn, was shaped by it. He was continually adjusting to new information, moving from one base of understanding to a new level of knowledge.

But knowledge alone is not wayfinding. How can you know the wind other than by sailing? The dance, other than by dancing? Wayfinding, other than by finding the way?

To know, Nainoa must sail.

He knew the stars and was somewhat acquainted with the sea. He needed a master teacher from whom he could learn the art of wayfinding. He wanted a teacher who could help him put it together in coherent form. For him there was one choice—Pius "Mau" Piailug.

Two Men, Two Ways

*M*au Piailug lives on a low coral island in the western Pacific with 600 other persons. Voyaging to distant islands is central to his culture's existence: "If my people didn't do this any more, we wouldn't be people any more."

Nainoa Thompson lives in a city on a high island in the middle of the Pacific with a million others and a half-million automobiles. For him, voyaging would be an act of self-affirmation. He needed a teacher. Mau was his only choice.

Late spring, 1979. For several weeks Nainoa had tried to get in touch with Mau by letter and by short-wave radio. When at last he heard that Mau was on Saipan and about to leave for Satawal, he set off from Honolulu to find him. When Mau, in turn, heard that Nainoa was on his way, he delayed his return to Satawal. A nonverbal sign from him, and his disciplined crew, attentive to such subtleties, pulled the canoe back onto shore to await Nainoa's arrival.

Nainoa was anxious about his meeting with the master. After all, the trip was costly and the uncertainty great. And Mau had said in 1976 that he would not be returning to Hawai'i.

The meeting was cordial and brief. Nainoa was surprised to find that Mau had remembered him from four years earlier. They sat together, talking quietly, waiting in silence. Mau was already committed to building a canoe on Puluwat. He smiled and gave no indication of what he might do. Nothing was there to give Nainoa any notion of the effectiveness of his mission. Perhaps Mau didn't himself know what he would do. Nothing written, nothing signed, and the half-hour meeting ended in a cordial farewell.

That brief encounter profoundly affected Nainoa. He came back a quieter person, more keenly aware of the power and complexity of nonverbal communication. A transformation had taken place and he was attuned to the beat of a most compelling drummer.

"Make Happy!" —Mau Piailug

"We're out here to learn . . ."
—Nainoa Thompson

Four months went by. Mau did not show nor did *Hōkūleʻa* sail. One day in late September Nainoa received a telephone call from the Honolulu airport that Mau and his son, Henry, were there waiting.

A few days later Harry Ho brought them all to the Bishop Museum Planetarium for Nainoa's first training session. Mau was delighted with the make-believe sky, chuckling at the absurdity in the instantaneous change from bright sunlight to the darkness of an air-conditioned starry night.

"Mailap, Merne, Maan," says Mau pointing out the stars he wants Nainoa to learn.

"Mailap, Merne, Maan," repeats Nainoa using Mau's names for the trio he knows as Altair, Vega, and Sirius.

"Sarapul, Aramoi, Balefang, Fyysemekyt," continues Mau pointing to Corvus, Arcturus, Ursa Minor, Polaris.

"Sarapul, Aramoi, Balefang, Fyysemekyt," responds Nainoa as if intoning a cabalistic chant.

Mau points out "storm stars," so fundamental in his system of navigation. Storm stars, Nainoa knows, form the basis of a calendar —a star's heliacal (coming up just ahead of the sun) appearance, a clue to events: a time for sailing, a time for planting, a time for repairing the canoe.

But storm stars are much more than that. Mau uses them in predicting the weather. "When Spica sets," he explains, "wind come from the west. Bring seven days good weather, seven days bad." The idea eludes Nainoa; he sees no causal relationship between the stars in the sky and weather on the planet. In fact, he wonders what interpretation is needed to assure congruency of prediction and event.

"When Sarapul come high we have good weather."

"How high?"

Mau hesitates. He knows how high is high.

Not Nainoa who presses with, "High as Fishmarket?" (Fyysemekyt, the North Star)

"No. Little bit higher I think. Then maybe we have bad weather."

"When? Next week? Will it be that high next week?"

"Yah, I think maybe next week," and Mau breaks into rapid talk with Henry, the interpreter.

Attempting to clarify, Nainoa asks, "When Merne is there . . . it goes from bad weather into good weather. Right?" Again Mau buzzes with Henry whose interpretation this time trails off into, "That makes strong the . . ."

A long quiet follows. Softly spoken words intermingle with silence. Are both parties withdrawing in an embarrassment of non-comprehension?

Mau uses only a few stars. Nainoa is surprised, for already he has well over a hundred in mind. That, in turn, surprises Mau. Is Mau's method so precise that he needs only a few? Or is wayfinding so deeply embedded in his being that he needs only a few?

Since Mau's wayfinding system requires much memorization, there's simply no point in memorizing more than you need. Developed by seafarers over generations of time and tested under all possible conditions, it combines the efficiency of engineering with the power of an art form and provides for all possible contingencies.

The precision and apparent casualness in Mau's navigating amazes Nainoa: "You have to be accurate in sailing from Saipan to Satawal, for Satawal is a low, coral island and hard to find. Accuracy must be in the star compass itself, not in star positions. I think Mau must compensate for the out-of-place stars. There's a system here but I don't understand it."

But Mau himself is not without his problems. The "storm star" system works well when he's in Satawal at a latitude of 7° north. However, here at 21° north he's surprised to find some stars rising before he expects them to. A 1–2–3 rising sequence in Satawal, for instance, might be a 2–1–3 event in Hawai'i due to a change in latitude. Either his system expands to incorporate the unusual or, simply, "No work here."

Mau talks of the importance of the navigator knowing ocean currents. Nainoa goes out to sea by himself in his small boat off the eastern end of O'ahu to learn of currents: "I'm beginning to know a current because when the wind is screaming and the current is flowing I feel uncomfortable. I lean into the wind and it feels as if the boat is coming out from under my feet."

Mau's ability to concentrate impresses Nainoa. They cross the 26-mile Moloka'i Channel in that small boat: "Mau is always looking at the sea. He doesn't talk much. You've got to concentrate to be a good navigator. You've got to be tense." He reflects for a moment and balances it with, "But you've got to relax." Still not satisfied, he changes "tense" to "intense," explaining, "because if I'm tense I get tired real fast."

He also finds Mau to have a great memory for navigational detail: "We go fishing. I put ten traps in the water and use landmarks to remember where they are. Bruce moves one when he's down under, but I don't know that he moved it. Next day we go back and Bruce cannot find it. Mau says, 'Over there.' We go look and there it is. It's uncanny. I don't know how he does it, but he just does it. I ask him if he knows where all the traps are and he says, 'No. One more time I know.'"

Late October. Nainoa has worked out a 36-point star compass that he'll later find need to simplify to 32 points. Even though he's understanding Mau's navigational system quite well, paradoxes persist. The concept of "equal spacing" is one. Three stars, for example, are setting. Two are close to each other and the third is set apart from the pair by a factor of two or more.

"Hey, Mau. These two stars . . . they more closer than these two?"

"Yes."

"They all equal spaced?"

"Yes."

Is it a lack of clear communication? A difference in the concept of equal? Or is Mau simply giving Nainoa the answer he thinks he wants? A long time will go by before the problem is resolved, when we find that Mau is thinking of "equal" in terms of value, not geometry. Two brothers in a family, for instance, are equal; so, too, may be chiefs of the same rank. And stars of unequal brightness and spacing may be of equal importance.

Is it better for Nainoa to use Mau's system without fully understanding it? Or should he stay with the system he has worked out and which he knows to be incomplete? "Do I go in March with what I have, because if I don't get Mau's method by then, where am I? I don't want to get caught between the two not understanding either. I want to be prepared, that's all."

Early November. The Research Committee of the Polynesian Voyaging Society meets at the Oceanic Institute on the windward side of

O'ahu in a conference room overlooking the sea—one of many planning sessions for the 1980 departure of *Hōkūle'a*. A short distance offshore is the dark basaltic island of Kāohikaipu. Beyond it is the whitish-buff tuff cone, Mānana Island. Drifting past the open doors of the institute are hang gliders heading for a landing on the sandy beach of Makapu'u, while cavorting in training tanks are sea mammals incessantly calling for attention. Here in the presence of these winged people, trainers of porpoises, and breeders of fish, Guy Rothwell resigns as chairman of the Research Committee and Dixon Stroup takes over. A hundred days and we'll be on our way.

Mid-November. Each morning Mau and Nainoa are going out to the Lāna'i Lookout at the eastern end of O'ahu to watch the morning happen. Nainoa is learning how to read the surface of the sea against the background of rising stars. "Mau doesn't say much. Sometimes nothing. We look, then we go back home. He tells me nothing. I have to ask."

Never before has Nainoa had such a teacher—no lesson plan, no agenda, no talk. His anxiety begins building in the silence of those early morning vigils. No manifest content. Nothing. Yet in silence was a message that took him a long time to catch: "Look."

Late November. I join them at the Lāna'i Lookout at 4:30 in the morning. Behind us, and blocking out the Honolulu city lights, is the hovering form of Koko Crater while directly overhead are Jupiter and Mars in Leo. Orion is setting.

The slaty-gray swell from the northeast crashes against the cliffs of Koko Head and bursts into whiteness. "That's Merne," says Mau as the water runs dark back to the sea.

Morning twilight tints high clouds, revealing at lower levels long, spearlike clouds over the channel. Beneath this channel cloud that tapers toward the southwest Mau is "looking for the wind" in a faint red haziness he calls "smoke." Hues are clues, subtle differences imperceptible to us but useful to him in predicting weather. Perhaps his language has words that precisely describe such delicate differences perceptible to him. We don't know. But we do know that his experience reveals to him a world that we must struggle to discern.

"No good for sail today, Nainoa," announces Mau. "Not too much smoke."

And that's today's lesson.

We go back to Nainoa's house on Bay Street. He fixes us a breakfast of eggs and sausage which he calls "nerves and tendons." We three sit on the floor drinking coffee and studying huge Chart 526 of the Pacific Ocean. Hawai'i is near the top of the chart, Tahiti near the bottom, and Satawal at the western edge. Nainoa has drawn many lines on the chart—straight ones, bent ones, zigzag ones, curved ones, saw-toothed ones. Hours of dreaming and calculating and vicarious sailing are in those lines. Here the implicit is explicit: we see what Nainoa has in mind.

Mau is fascinated with maps and charts. And even though he might not be able to read the words, he knows where the islands are on paper and how to find them in the sea. We study the course he sailed in 1976—the masterful stroke—along with symbols representing wind direction and strength, magnetic fields, distances, ocean depths, currents.

"Eh, Mau, what about the Cooks? Gordon like go Cooks."

Mau studies the chart and says nothing.

Nainoa has worked on the problem. Countless times. He slides a huge 45° triangle over the chart and continues, "Getting to the Cooks from Tahiti is easy, a piece of cake. It's downwind. Four or five days maybe. Coming back is hard—right into the trades all the way." His zigzag tacking course shows the return trip might take twenty-eight days.

"I think maybe thirty days," says Mau.

"Mau! We go Cooks, come back Satawal."

Mau chuckles, for Satawal is so far downwind that the idea is preposterous. Returning to Hawai'i from Satawal would require sailing three thousand miles directly into the wind. He uses a match box and his hand to demonstrate the absurdity of such a long tack. "Go this way . . . go that way . . . this way . . . that way . . . stay forever same!" Like Sisyphus doomed to his eternal task of getting nowhere.

We talk of *etak*, a word that Mau uses in expressing distance traveled in terms of the changing bearing of a reference island. The canoe in this frame of reference is taken as being at rest in the center of a circle. Islands move at the circle's edge as the wind fills the canoe's sails. It's not a belief, of course, but a way of processing information, a way of visualizing, a way of solving a problem. Right now *etak* has little meaning for Nainoa. "What makes sense to me is that Mau uses *etak* to make landfall. If you don't catch the wind right, the islands will be moving too fast and you'll miss your destination."

Mid-December. Four-thirty in the morning and we three go out to Koko Head. Mau sits in the back seat of the car saying not a word. All three of us are silent. What is there to say? Nothing. So we ride on in silence.

We stop at the Lāna'i Lookout and walk over to the stone wall. Mau looks up at the stars and out to sea and says nothing. He stands firmly, arms folded across his chest, feet well apart in a solid stance he so often assumes on the canoe at sea. It's warm this morning and he's wearing red trunks and no shirt.

Nainoa stands tall and thin. Draped over his shoulders and extending down to his feet is a bedspread. In this dim light he's a grand, regal person of old in feather cape but without the traditional feather helmet. For the past few days he has been experimenting with getting along on less sleep. Today he's wearing his sleep-deprivation experiment, so I have an idea why he's quiet.

Mars and Jupiter are completing the first event of a triple conjunction. I break the silence by pointing to the waning gibbous moon and saying, "Sunday the moon will be passing close to Jupiter." Mau stretches out his arm, spreads his fingers, and counts, "Friday . . . Saturday . . . Sunday." He nods, chuckles; and I'm happy for having my prediction confirmed by so eminent a wayfinder.

Mau is a short, powerful man—a gentle man. We watch the color appearing in the sky and in quiet, musical intonation he suddenly says, "Not too much wind today, Nainoa."

"How you know?"

"Clouds not move too fast. No more smoke." He's comparing stored images of ten thousand sunrises he has in mind with what's out there.

"No more smoke," repeats Nainoa.

Pleased with his student's progress Mau smiles and recaps the learning, "Not too much wind today, Nainoa."

Teacher and student, master and apprentice—there they are standing together before the advancing sun. A dawn scene, enacted throughout the ages, here being re-enacted on the slopes of Koko Head. Intellectual kinship is being affirmed in silence, values perpetuated in morning twilight. Here are the searchers, the knowers, the keepers of the secret—one attired in red trunks and the other in a bedspread.

"Not too much wind today, Nainoa!"

Into the Smoke

*L*ate December. Nainoa thinks it might be good for me to experience the "smoke" in the Moloka'i Channel.

We meet in the darkness of Niu Valley at 4:30 A.M. and climb into a rusty pickup truck with an oversized Mustang engine. It takes a big engine to pull this 23-foot boat on its trailer. We drive slowly along Kalaniana'ole Highway, eastward against the car lights of the earliest Honolulu commuters and out onto the sandy bay-mouth bar of Kuapā. Nainoa backs the trailer down the concrete ramp into the water, loosens the lines, and the boat is afloat.

He starts its engines and we buzz out of the harbor. Channel markers are flying by on both sides as I recall the old mnemonic, "Red, right, returning." I check and find the red markers on the left. "Good, he knows what he's doing!"

We bounce along, sometimes leaping from the top of one wave to another, sometimes landing solidly in a trough. I hold tightly to the railing beneath the spray shield and keep my knees flexed to absorb the shock of impact. Lots of power in this boat with its twin engines revved up. Bearded Nainoa, pivoting from his ankles, leans onto the wheel as he coaxes the boat up and over the waves. He's relaxed and comfortable. Even though I'm neither of the two, still I do rather enjoy the experience. We speed along, bouncing, pitching, tossing, falling. Occasionally he glances in my direction and I feel cared for.

We're in the "smoke." Today the spearlike clouds are right above us. Nainoa orients himself: "Makapu'u Light House and Rabbit [Mānana] Island make a good north-south line. Here in the channel it's easy; we've got landmarks. But out in the open sea and far from land, there's nothing. We've also got backwash from the cliffs and the funneling effect of the channel to deal with. Farther out, we get the deep ocean swells; they're easier to read."

Nainoa cuts the engine and we drift on a black ocean. He sits on the engine housing, propping one foot against the gunwale, a solid stance in the rocking waves. I hang onto the railing and watch. He's so easy with the sea out here, as easy as I am with a planetarium machine on land.

Facing east, he points his right arm along the horizon to where he expects the sun to rise and swings his left arm toward Polaris. Then he stretches both arms upward as if to feel the spacing between the crescent moon and Hōkūleʻa (Arcturus). So oriented, he turns his attention to the sea.

Taking a compass from his pocket, he checks the direction of the swells. "Oh," he sighs, "20° off." To that note of despair I add, "And how will you ever find Tahiti?" Later we check the compass and find that it had not been adjusted properly so that his error was less than 10°, a figure quite acceptable in conditions here in the channel.

"See that swell coming from the east? That's Mailap." Mailap is the Satawalese name for the star Altair, rising almost directly east.

Then he points to another swell coming from the northeast: "Mau calls it Merne. That's the northeast swell and it's always there." He uses Mau's star names for direction. Later he'll give Hawaiian names to these directions on his star compass.

Bulbous tops of cumulus clouds turn pink as the sun appears far to the south of east at this time of winter solstice. Three months from now at the time of the vernal equinox it will be rising directly east. Where will we be then? In the countercurrent? The doldrums? At the equator?

"The swell from the south is small. It's coming from very far away. Either that or it may never have been strong to begin with."

The sun is well into the sky, and the swell directions for the day have been determined. Again the engines roar and we head for home. Koko Head grows in size, and from this angle its sloping beds of consolidated volcanic ash give the appearance of the whole structure sliding off into the sea. A large sea cave at its base is a smoothly rounded pothole curving upward and outward. "You cannot see that cave from the land," explains Nainoa, "because the sea cliffs are too steep. Only way of seeing it is from the sea."

Koko Head is the scene of Nainoa's early encounters with the sea.

Often as a lad he'd hike up the ridge and jump off the cliffs into the sea to float happily and knowingly for long periods of time in the active waves. Close to this sea cave is a smaller one with a low ceiling. It traps the waves, compresses the air, and whooshes white spray back onto the sea.

Birds are circling. Nainoa has been studying them, "the way they fly in formation with their leader setting the pace and direction with four flaps and a glide." Birds lead the wayfinder to the land.

Red channel markers are speeding by on the right as we enter the canal. While he's securing the boat, I go to a fast-food place to pick up breakfast. By the time I get back to his house he has already finished plotting today's swell observations on the star compass.

It has been a good morning. Nainoa is confident. He's ready for the voyage, and in a wistful moment asks, "What are we going to do when the voyage is all over?"

"Oh, you'll be a master wayfinder then." He smiles when I acknowledge his striving for competence while longing for innocence by adding, "But the job market really isn't all that great."

"Be patient with me. I'm not Mau. Take away the sun and stars and I have a hard time. I'm a learner, not a navigator."

Increasing Momentum

*T*wo days before Christmas 1979. *Hōkūleʻa*'s sails are spread out on the parking lot beside the Harbor Pilot Boat House at Pier 12 in downtown Honolulu. Two brightly painted outrigger canoes are at the seaward end of the pier, and at the other end big semitrucks go whizzing by, raising dust on Nimitz Highway.

A few weeks ago the sails were removed and reshaped to make them more suitable for the 1980 voyage. Our task today is that of tying the sails to their wooden supporting members and installing them at the masts. Short lines are run through brass grommets at the edges of the sails, around the gaff (the vertical member running parallel to the mast) or around the boom (the curved piece that holds the sail open, giving it the crab-claw form), then tied off in square knots.

Mau watches. Beneath his green visored baseball cap is his brown face and easy smile. Today he's wearing his favorite tank-top shirt with "Copperfield's Pub" stenciled on the back. His son, Henry Piailug, stands apart. A broad-brimmed cowboy hat shades his face. With ample hat and dark visage he might just have come off the range.

Weekend sailing is vital to crew training. Not only does it give crew members experience in handling a double-hulled canoe, it also gives them a way of learning how others respond to a variety of sailing conditions.

Eight crew members shoulder the forward boom and gaff with the new sail attached, carry it aboard the canoe and place it in the socket at the forward mast. Lines are secured and Mike Tongg asks Mau, "This one you like for pull now?" Mau nods. Boom and gaff pivot into position.

Anthony Guerrero at the steering sweep of *Hōkūleʻa*

73

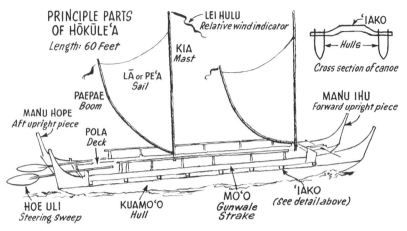

Principle parts of the double-hulled canoe

"Tricing lines too low," is Leon Sterling's terse comment. "Gotta go more up." But in the process of going "more up" the lines tangle, and Nainoa shinnies up the mast to release them.

Water has entered the watertight compartments. Marion Lyman disappears into one compartment and reappears with a bucket of water. She spills it onto the deck, and while the water is running out the scuppers she descends for another bucket. Several bobbings and she emerges with a triumphant declaration, "Six in that one."

A misty golden rain is falling on Honolulu. It's spilling from the clouds hugging the crest of the Koʻolau mountains five miles up Nuʻuanu Valley. The wind is light but we'll have a good sailing day. We know that because Mau and Nainoa saw "good smoke" early this morning from the Lānaʻi Lookout.

Three hours of preparation and *Hōkūleʻa* is ready to sail. We gather in a circle, join hands and bow our heads as Mike offers a *pule* seeking safety and protection for those aboard and relating today's training to a broader perspective.

"Stand by to cast off!"

Nainoa is standing on the floating platform to which *Hōkūleʻa* is moored. Tony Guerrero is with him. I'm down on the canoe along with the rest of the crew. Nainoa motions to me and I pull on a line. I feel important. Helpful. I pull smartly and nothing happens. My eyes follow the line to a deck cleat that is also firmly fastened to

Leon Sterling, hand on a steering sweep, guiding *Hōkūleʻa* out of Honolulu Harbor

Hōkūleʻa. No amount of tugging on that line, however smartly, will get us underway. Slowly I raise my eyes. Nainoa is standing straight and tall, gazing patiently out to sea. Is that a slight grin I see on his face?

Lines slacken and we begin moving away from the pier. Tony casts off the last line and makes a magnificent leap from the platform onto the rapidly departing canoe. His timing is perfect and his deftness receives cheers from an appreciative crew.

The 40-horsepower engine, used for maneuvering in the harbor, is lowered. Leon Sterling straddles the engine and steers it with his feet, leaning from side to side as he does so to see around parts of the canoe that obstruct his view. He's an uncommon cowboy commanding forty horses from beneath a high deck of a double-hulled canoe. Blue exhaust fumes swirl around him and a light blue kerchief protects his hairless head. His rugged frame is naked down to his waist, and at his hairy chest glistens a *Hōkūleʻa* medallion on a golden chain.

Hatch covers are secured with large rubber-band "bungees." Jo-

Anne Sterling washes down the deck, for there are always house-keeping chores aboard the canoe. We move alongside the big boulders at the end of Sand Island and begin catching the roll of the deep ocean swells. Nainoa motions, and the crew brings down the forward boom. Wind pockets in the sail and we take off. The stern lifts out of the water; the outboard propeller spins wildly and ineffectively in the air. Man and machine come aboard. The engine is secured to the deck and Leon goes about his never-ending task of attending to the condition of the vessel.

A good wind moves us out along Ala Moana Beach. We're 5 miles off Waikīkī when I point to a swell coming from the southeast and ask Nainoa, "Is that Tumur?" (Tumur is Mau's name for the star Antares, a red giant rising east of southeast.)

"Hard to tell out here because the waves are being bent by the land. When we get farther out we'll see the deep-ocean swells."

We talk of sea and swells, for it is in learning the motion of the ocean that the wayfinder is able to maintain orientation. Swells are the big waves generated by pressure systems, such as the trade winds. They stretch from horizon to horizon and maintain direction for months at a time. Seas, on the other hand, are locally generated waves superimposed upon the prevailing swells.

From what appears to us as a chaotic array of waves, Mau Piailug discerns meaning. He reads that which eludes us and uses it in maintaining continuous orientation. So it is, in the wayfinder's ability to read and interpret nature's signs, that survival of oceanic culture is preserved.

"Can you feel the waves?" I ask.

"Only when I'm looking at them, so it isn't really by feel. Mau can, though. He can be below deck and sort out the swells by the feel of the canoe."

We study canoe performance. The crew moves forward. Weight, balance, and the center of gravity all shift and that affects canoe handling. "Direction now 110°," reports architect Harry Ho. "That's a 15° change from when the crew was aft." He's taking bearings with a compass as a way for better understanding of the relationship between the loading of the canoe and its capability of pointing into the wind.

By now we're well out from land, heading toward Moloka'i, and someone spontaneously blends the spirit of the season with the joy of sailing in a fervent rendition of, "I'll be home for Christmas." A spirit less sanguine hopes it will be sooner.

Mau sits on the port hull of *Hōkūle'a* eating Saloon Pilot crackers as he watches the sea. A high-peaking wave breaks against the canoe and he scrambles to avoid a drenching. Not quite fast enough. He gets doused and laughs. His quick movement seems to show that he's ahead in his bout with the gout. Yesterday Nainoa took him to the doctor to get some pills. I empathize with Mau on his condition, and he massages my shoulders. Here's a thoughtful, a truly gentle, man. No wonder the crew admires him. In this simple expression of compassion I know why he's loved and respected.

Where the Tumur swell meets the Mailap swell, we come about and move along the southern shore of O'ahu into the afternoon sun, taking turns at the steering sweeps. Dipping these long-

Wally Froiseth attending to the relashing of *Hōkūle'a*

handled paddles into the water from either starboard or port hull, or from the center of the canoe, creates a temporary keel. The wind drives the canoe in one direction, the sweeps exert a counter force. A combination of brisk trade winds moving 6 tons of canoe with human muscle and sheer exuberence cracks one of the sweeps. Since such repairs are not readily made at sea, Canoe Committee Chairman Wally Froiseth will either fix it in the shop or make a new one. Much is yet to be learned.

We've had a good four hours of training. Sails are triced (folded against the mast). The engine is lowered and Leon is back in the saddle again. He guides us past the Bishop Museum's large square-rigged vessel, *Falls of Clyde,* past the ornately gold-trimmed red-and-green Chinese floating restaurant, *Oceania,* then along the Matson dock where long-necked, long-legged cranes that look like praying mantises attend to unloading container ships. Two tug boats are turning the *Sohio Resolute* tanker in the harbor, leaving us little room for maneuvering. An anxious moment it is, with *Hōkūleʻa*'s engine sputtering, but Leon is equal to the challenge.

The canoe is secured, the gear is stowed, and the sun is lighting the clouds over the Waiʻanae range. *Hōkūleʻa* bobs quietly at its mooring after a busy day at sea. And now it's "talk-story" time. A waxing gibbous moon is rising and our spirits along with it. A moon dance is in order. So we improvise one, honoring the rising and setting and phasing of this noble "Queen of the Night"—honoring it right there on the parking lot at Pier 12 beside the Harbor Pilot Boat House in downtown Honolulu.

Mid-January. *Hōkūleʻa* moves into Snug Harbor on Sand Island for drydocking. The "worm shoe" on the bottom of each hull needs replacing and a separation between deck and gunwale must be caulked. A steel cradle is run down an inclined railway and into the water. The canoe is fitted to it and secured. Then a large electric engine pulls the cable and *Hōkūleʻa* rides the rails out of the water and into a huge open shed with a corrugated iron roof. Twenty small boats will keep it company in the Amfac Marina. Most are fat, single-hulled boats with deep keels. One is named *Arcturus* after the star from which *Hōkūleʻa* also takes its name.

A small boatyard is a place for caring, a place where hours of

It takes two workers at each station to lash the deck of the canoe

human effort—repairing, replacing, smoothing, painting, sanding, and stroking—are bestowed upon inanimate objects. Somehow in the ambivalence of caring you begin loving that which takes so much of your time. The haul-out intensifies the dream.

The bamboo deck of *Hōkūle‘a* has been splintering and must be replaced. Strips of fir replace them and they are lashed to the crossbeams. Dacron line is threaded over and under the fir and around the crossbeams in a pattern both ornamental and sturdy. A worker on deck feeds the line through holes to one below who threads it around the crossbeam and back into the deck. After each turn the line is cinched up tight—*zing tight,* to conform to Mau's criterion of excellence in that art.

Sanding and scraping the hull is dusty work requiring the use of masks. Applying antifouling paint has its hazards and the fumes of fiberglassing are but momentarily intriguing. Each person has a part

Marlene Among, executive secretary of the Polynesian Voyaging Society

Marion Lyman, wondering if getting there is half the fun

in readying *Hōkūleʻa* for the sea. A spirit of camaraderie develops among the workers, many of whom are working only because they believe in the project, knowing that they'll not be making the trip.

While *Hōkūleʻa* is still in drydock Nainoa flies to Tahiti to study the stars and to make arrangements for the canoe's arrival in the spring. A few days later Mau and I head for Singapore to do a scene on pre-Western navigation in the Pacific for a television documentary, "The Commanding Sea."

Mau Piailug

Singapore Swing

Mau and I are 40,000 feet above the Pacific, traveling at 500 miles an hour toward Singapore. It's an eleven-hour flight from Honolulu to Hong Kong, then another three to Singapore. The flight attendant passes out pillows and earphones and we settle back to listen to jazz, comedy, symphony, or rock. Hot towels and snacks appear. I look at Mau and wonder how he's doing.

He goes to sleep. It's four in the morning on this prolonged day. We're flying west. Each hour stretches into an hour and a half as we race the sun at half its speed. A slow sunrise, a long day. But it will be a short day, too, for soon we'll be crossing the International Date Line to enter the day after tomorrow today. Mau looks so comfortable, his head resting on a pillow in the corner by the window, earphones sliding off his head. Time to wake up for breakfast.

The plane is flying in full sunlight while the ocean below is still in darkness. Creeping downward, the sunlight reveals long lanes of tilted-back trade wind clouds like those we've seen so many times over the Moloka'i Channel. I wonder how it seems to Mau to be looking down, not up, at the dawning of a day. Chin on hand, he studies the scene.

The pleasant flight attendant leans over Mau to pull down the window blind. Surprised by the movement, Mau looks up at her. She explains softly that it is time for the movie and that people cannot see the screen with the shade up. Mau smiles comprehendingly and responds, "Too much light?" She smiles and nods, and the Pacific Ocean that he knows so well disappears behind plastic. The movie is a fantasy-comedy of a motorcyclist tearing up the southwestern American desert while frustrated police officers in hot pursuit inadvertently tip over their cars. He watches for a while and drifts off to sleep.

We're a thousand miles closer to Asia as the film ends. I'm dozing as the blinds are raised. Light floods in, and I'm startled by Mau's imperative, "Will, look!" Far below he sees islands appearing and disappearing beneath tufts of trade wind clouds. Coral islands they are, like those in the Carolines he knows so well.

"Oh," I say, not yet able to see them. He counts, "Three . . . four . . . five . . . six islands." I stand up and lean over him to look. Clouds and sea, that's all I see. No islands. He sees them. I don't.

Where in the world are we? We must be too far north for those to be his island group, the Carolines. Are we flying a great circle route? If so, we must be well north of Saipan, and those islands could be in the Marianas. Or maybe they're islands near Iwo Jima. At any rate, the technology that gets us here does not tell us where we are.

I draw a circle on a piece of paper. "Here's the earth." Mau has no trouble with that abstraction. "Here's Honolulu . . . Satawal . . . Singapore." He nods. I continue, "Sun's flying with us. We're flying half as fast as the sun."

"Long day," is his quiet understanding.

Now a bigger circle. "It's 4,000 miles from the center of earth to the outside." He nods. "We're six miles high. Maybe seven. Deepest place in ocean is the same as we are high—the Mariana Trench, north of the Carolines."

We look out the window at the line of sea and sky. "From this high up the horizon is 250 miles." I draw tangents to that circle. "But from the deck of *Hōkūleʻa* it's three, maybe four miles."

Mau may or may not be following what I'm saying. Somehow that's not important to me. What is important is that this is a moment of sharing our knowledge—his of finding islands that I cannot see, and mine of making the world a circle with lines running off in tangents.

Asia feels closer. Clouds are stacking higher. "Clouds look like ice," says Mau. Ice? Like icebergs in the sea? Where has he seen ice? He lives 7° north of the equator and his travels have never taken him into polar regions. Neither have mine. Yet he knows. He's comparing stored mental images of photographs with what he sees below. So am I, and the clouds do look like ice.

The DC-10 glides over Hong Kong Bay. Mau slides down in his

seat to peer upward at apartment houses stacked along cliffs and moving past us at a great rate. While the plane is refueling we wander among the shops in the airport. An hour later we're having lunch six miles above the South China Sea—a sea upon which we'll soon find are twentieth-century pirates. We land in Singapore, check in at the Hilton and enter another world of splendor.

Next morning Mau is up at four, sitting quietly and watching the stars. After a half hour's silence he bursts out with, "Going to be a good day today, Will."

"How you know?"

"Wind in the north."

"Oh."

The Big Dipper at this time is low in the northwestern sky. We cannot see the North Star for we're at the equator and it's at the horizon. Mintaka has made its zenith passage over Singapore and has already set. "Two months from now," I say showing my learning, "we'll be back beneath Mintaka as we cross the equator on our way to Tahiti." He grunts, and I sense that my erudition was not necessary.

"Where's Tumur?" (Antares)

He tosses his head, points with his thumb, and laughs, "Behind hotel."

Of course! We're facing north and Tumur rises in the southeast. Mau is oriented wherever he is.

Breakfast is wheeled into our room on a stainless steel cart. Silver domes cover plates of scrambled eggs and sausage. Coffee is served in a silver pot. Beneath another silver dome lies whole-wheat toast, and a splendid array of silver implements is ours to use. We eat and say nothing.

Later we meet with Michael Gill, producer and director of the six-part documentary, "The Commanding Sea." He is keenly aware of the fragility of the sea and the importance of balancing technological change with preservation. His productions for the BBC and cinema have won virtually every major international award. "Civilization" with Lord Kenneth Clark and "America" with Alistair Cooke are among his better-known works.

Clare Francis joins us. She will do the continuity and write a book about the film. A small, courageous, and intensely feminine woman, Clare has twice sailed alone across the Atlantic. Once she commanded an eleven-member crew on a round-the-world race. Educated at the Royal Ballet School in London, she received a degree in economics at London University and has written two books on her sailing experiences.

Our task this morning is that of going out to the *Golden Hind* with the film crew, then in the afternoon to a sandy beach where Mau will demonstrate his wayfinding method as representative of pre-Western navigation in the Pacific.

A small rubber boat powered by an outboard engine picks us up, and we bounce out to the *Golden Hind,* a replica of the ship that Sir Francis Drake used three centuries ago in sailing around the world. Black hull, thick rope ladders, and shroud lines covered with black tallow combine to give it a sinister look. Heavy masts, high super-structure, and large white sails with red crosses create a pirate ship of old. This ominous anachronism seems large; yet it is only 64 feet long at the water line, about the same as *Hōkūleʻa.*

Drake was known for his marauding ventures, particularly against the Spanish. Ironically, aboard this modern pirate ship of old are sand-bag installations, antiboarding nets, and automatic rifles to stave off the threat of piracy that still exists on the high seas of the twentieth century.

We walk bent over in the galley to avoid the heavy beams. Stoves mounted on rafters are free to swing as the vessel moves—actually to remain where they are as the ship rolls beneath. We spend much of our time in the galley out of camera range talking with the "Golden Boys," a term that Drake himself used, so befitting these blond young men from England.

The Golden Boys tend the ship, scurrying up and down rope ladders, edging out along the manrails, leaning over the spars to furl the sails. Occasionally we lend a hand, pulling on the lines to swing the heavy spars from one direction to another so that the ship can come about and head back toward the camera.

Mau has never been on a square-rigger before. Neither have I. I'm impressed and expect him also to be intrigued. He's fascinated for a while, for this is a different way of moving over the sea from what he's used to, but there is no mystery here for him. He understands what's going on and how it works and turns to watch the sea he knows so well, studying the swells in this place of large islands at the edge of a continent.

Filming of the *Golden Hind* ends. We step into the rubber dinghy and bounce back to shore. The film crew travels in another boat and we all converge on a sandy beach in Singapore.

Mau prepares to demonstrate his star compass. We gather shells and coconuts and bits of drift material. He draws a circle in the sand to represent the horizon. On its edge he places shells for stars, and at the center a coconut for the canoe. Cameras and sound equipment move in and we're ready for action.

Clare, a diminutive five-foot superwoman, and genial Mau sit together on the sand looking at the shell-studded circle. A crewman writes on a chalkboard,"MAU—TAKE 1," and holds it in front of Mau's chest. He looks down at it, then up at Clare. Her nod reassures him that this abrupt action is okay; the camera whirs and the interview begins.

"Did you like the *Golden Hind?*" asks Clare with a smile.

"Yes."

"Is it like your boat?"

"No."

Mau laughs and shakes his head at the absurdity of such a comparison. He appears to be so at ease, enjoying Clare's line of questioning as well as the antics of the film crew. He's quiet, not at all shy, an actor sitting in the sand and telling of his art. Each of Clare's questions he returns with a smile and a happy monosyllable. No elaboration. No qualification. And how is Clare going to get a documentary out of this?

"Mau, from whom did you learn navigation?"

"My father and my grandfather teach me." Good, now we're getting somewhere.

"And how old were you then?" Mau begins his reply as a long wooden boat with a loud engine putts into close range. A man wearing a large Chinese coolie hat is piloting it. He is looking out to sea and quite unaware of the part of the filming he has become. A crewman claps his hinged chalkboard with his message on it, the camera stops, and we wait for the boat to go out of range.

"MAU—TAKE 2." Clare nods and Mau continues, "I'm six years old when I start to learn. I am sixteen when I sail to other islands." A 747 climbs into the sky from Singapore Airport, and its roaring engines cause the hinged chalkboard once again to snap like alligator jaws. We wait. Beads of perspiration stand out on Mau's forehead in this hot mid-afternoon sun at the equator. He doesn't seem to mind, though, for he's a happy teacher sitting in the sand and talking navigation.

"MAU—TAKE 3." Clare begins, "How old were you when you began to learn . . ." and the putt-putt-putt of a helicopter causes the chalkboard jaws once more to snap.

"MAU—TAKE 4." We begin a long session, this one without interruption. Mau speaks in English although she encourages him to use Satawalese if he finds it more comfortable, and later they would dub in a translation.

"Stars are first," says Mau. "They teach me first about the stars. Then they teach me about the islands."

He places a small coconut at the center of the circle representing a canoe at sea. Shells on the rim mark the rising and setting places of particular stars. So close are the shells to each other that some are touching, and I wonder if they represent sectors to his mind rather than discrete points on the compass. If so, it sheds light on that persistent problem of "inequality" in the equal spacing of stars.

"This is Merne . . . come up here . . . go down here," says Mau moving a shell in an arc across the circle from east to west. "Here's Tumur . . . come up here . . . go down here." How beautiful the concept, how teachable the star compass!

"But how do you steer when you cannot see the stars?"

"I use the wave. Big wave come sometime from Merne," and he places the midrib of a coconut frond on the circle to show a line of swells coming from the northeast.

"Big wave come from Tumur," and another midrib indicates the southeast swell. The two intersect in a recognizable pattern—peaks and troughs on the sea that he has pointed out so often to *Hōkūleʻa* crews in training sessions off Oʻahu.

A circle is the horizon and a coconut is the canoe. Shells are stars and midribs are swells. Displayed here on the sands of Singapore is a navigational system that enabled ancient peoples to move out of Asia and into Oceania thousands of years ago.

While camera and microphone are being set up for the final scene, Clare asks me, "What else shall I cover?"

"Get into the transmission of knowledge," I respond quickly. "That's how he learned. Chant is central in a culture of oral tradition."

"MAU—TAKE 5." Clare leads, "And how do you remember all this?"

Beautiful! Here's a perfect set-up for a reply that will give credit to chant!

"Oh," says Mau, surprised with the innocent simplicity of the question, "I learn it in my head."

The camera closes in for a final question, "And how many stars are there in your system?"

Again with disarming directness he responds, "Plenty."

Slowly the camera backs away, swinging its view toward the sea and then along the shore to catch Clare, now standing on a big camera box, gazing up into a palm tree.

Next afternoon Mau and I are at the Singapore airport two hours ahead of departure time and ready for that long trip back to Honolulu.

"Your passport, please." The attendant "chops" mine and looks worried about Mau's.

"Where's your visa?" Mau does not understand.

Gracious but firm the attendant says, "You cannot leave Singapore without a visa." I explain that Mau is a resident of the Trust Territories and that he needs no visa to get into the United States. True, if he's entering from Micronesia, but it is becoming all too clear that Mau cannot leave Singapore without a U.S. visa.

"You'll have to go to the American Embassy, but you cannot get back in time for this plane."

We're stuck in Singapore.

I'm anxious. I feel a need to hurry to the Embassy even though there's no need for speed with at least a day of waiting ahead of us, maybe more. Still I'm anxious. I wish I weren't, but I am. A taxi stops to unload a bearded man and his portly wife, an unhappy looking couple. I ask the cab driver if he'll take us to the Embassy.

"Yes." We get into the cab and the driver unloads the luggage.

The big man with lots of luggage glances sharply from the cab driver to me. His eyes are jumpy and he seems to be swelling up. I think he feels slighted, as if we've pre-empted the cab. While Mau and I are seated in the taxi and waiting for the driver to unload the luggage, the big man pulls open the door, looks fiercely past Mau and glares at me. His eyes are large and his gray beard trembles as he shouts, "This is *not* the only cab in Singapore!" He closes the door. The cab rocks.

"What's the matter?" asks Mau, mystified by such behavior. I explain that it's anxiety on both our parts—on his to catch a plane and on mine to get to the Embassy. But the amount of anger and its mode of expression baffles Mau. In attempting to comprehend this public temper tantrum, he can only shake his head and say, "He no make happy." Still mystified, he'll ask about it at dinner that night, again the following morning, and once more on our glide path into Honolulu.

We're on our own in Singapore and find a modest hotel. Lucky we are, for people are already beginning to arrive for the Chinese New Year celebration and rooms are not easy to get.

After dinner we wander around the streets of Singapore near the hotel. Mau needs a belt to hold up his sagging trousers. We enter a clothing store, a high-pressure merchandising operation. I'm wary lest Mau be "taken," but he isn't. He buys a belt of good quality, also a wallet, smiles at the shopkeeper and we leave.

We return to the hotel room. I read to him from Ben Finney's book *Pacific Navigation and Voyaging,* a collection of papers on navigation by a variety of authors. Mau is mentioned several times in Mike McCoy's article on Carolinian navigation, along with the Satawalese brothers Repunglung and Repunglap who began a resurgence in long-distance sailing.

It's a strange scene. Here we are on the seventh floor of a hotel in Singapore. I'm looking at configurations of words in a book, evoking sounds from patterns in print that are strange to Mau—sounds that describe a world of coral islands and outriggers that I know little about, while Mau corrects my pronunciation of sounds that conjure up in his mind images and memories of home.

An article by Saul Riesenberg on Puluwat navigation names the islands in the Caroline group: "Puluwat, Pulusuk, Tamatam, Pulap, Ulul . . ." Mau looks over my shoulder and joins the recitation, "Magur, Ono, Onari, Piseras . . ." I thought he couldn't read.

He can't, but we continue in unison, "East Fayu, Nomwin,

Fananu, Truk, Oroluk, Ponape . . ." The list is his legacy, a tie with a past he keeps alive through chant. And when intoned, those symbols illumine stored information.

"Kosrae, Ngatik, Lukunor, Ta . . ." The story is that of a parrotfish living in a deep hole in the Puluwat reef. A probing stick frightens the fish and it flees to a reef hole in another island, Pulusuk. Each time the stick threatens, the fish swims on to another island, "Satawan, Mor, Kutu, Namoluk . . ." And after visiting all the islands it returns—to Puluwat.

Mau knows many chants and he has committed great masses of information to memory. His "ocean in mind" is studded with hundreds of little islands. He knows winds and currents. And he knows how to enter reefs by using both real and imaginary markers. An imaginary figure is that of three golden plovers circling a frigate bird. So, too, the spirit who lives in a flame, and a man standing in a canoe made of ferns.

Metaphor rich in imagery, a delightful way of remembering vast amounts of detail. Perhaps the closest we get to such ways of thinking is in imagining certain points of light in our sky as forming the half-man half-horse monster, Sagittarius, or a half-goat half-fish creature, Capricornus.

Mau's esoteric navigational knowledge includes content in several categories, identified by Riesenburg as: Reef Hole Probing, Catching the Sea Bass, the Sail of Limahacha, Aligning the Weir, Looking at an Island, the Great Trigger Fish, Ayufal's Tail, Aligning the Skids, the Fortune Telling of the Sea Bass' Food, the Torch of the Lagoon of Anuufa, the Lashing of the Breadfruit Picker.

Next morning Mau is up at four, quietly watching the dawning of a new day.

"Good this day today, Will."

"Yes," I respond showing yesterday's learning. "Wind is in the north."

Mau smiles, tosses his head and motions with his thumb. "Tumur behind hotel," and we laugh.

And it *is* a good day. The Embassy clears us quickly and we're able to get the last two seats on the plane; however, departure is delayed ten hours and it is midnight before we leave.

Mau Piailug

A thin crescent moon in an intensely blue sky is riding close to a crimson horizon on the dawning of this short day. Tomorrow there will be no moon at all for it's Chinese New Year, the time of New Moon. What a splendid scene! We're high above the Pacific and heading eastward for a most beautiful sight—the sun rising out of the Pacific. To witness such an event, devout pilgrims in Japan climb to the top of Fujiyama. And in Hawai'i determined motorists begin driving at three in the morning to the summit of the shield volcano Haleakalā, to witness the sunrise spectacle from the "house of the sun."

We're lucky, for we're three times higher than either of those two volcanic edifices and above most of the water vapor on this planet. Blue and red are intensifying as the sun is about to appear. With so sharp a horizon we ready ourselves for the phenomenon of green flash—the sun's green rim appearing a fraction of a second ahead of the sun's reddened disk.

Wait . . . any moment now . . .

But it's time for the movie. Window blinds come down. Once more sun, moon, and Pacific disappear behind plastic. And it's that same movie—that one about the motorcyclist tearing up the southwestern American desert while frustrated police officers in hot pursuit inadvertently tip over their cars—and we miss the dawning of a short day.

Sunrise and sunset are but a few hours apart as we meet the sun at 1,500 miles an hour. Mau watches sea and sky for hours, endlessly fascinated with the changing scene. Then he dozes. Is the gout bothering him? He has his pills. Nainoa has seen to that, but I don't know whether he's been taking them.

How strange the Singapore experience must have been for him! Certainly it was for me, for in it I saw more clearly than ever before ways in which culture shapes our thinking.

We're on our glide path into Honolulu. Mau is looking over my shoulder as I fill out his custom declaration form. Once more he asks, "What was that man mad about?"

Strategy

By now, Nainoa had a wayfinding system that could be used anywhere and a particular strategy for finding Tahiti. He had devised a star compass, he had learned of wind and sea conditions he might find along the way, and he was familiar with the birds that could help in expanding landfall.

THE STAR COMPASS

Nainoa had developed a compass for staying oriented, basing it on the rising and setting positions of stars along the horizon. He used the established Hawaiian names for the cardinal points of direction:

Hikina   East, "coming," the direction from which the sun comes into the sky

Komohana   West, "to enter," the direction in which the sun enters the sea

ʻĀkau   North, "right," to the right of the observer facing west, the direction of the sun's path across the sky

Hema   South, "left," to the left of the observer facing west, the direction of the traveling sun.

Nainoa's first compass had thirty-six divisions, each of 10°. He wanted as many divisions as practicable for precision, as few as necessary for efficiency.

His second compass reduced that number to thirty-two. Each of the four quadrants he divided in half, giving the directions of northeast, southeast, southwest, and northwest. He got the idea from Mau, a more "natural" division of the horizon since the prevailing

Marlene Among at the port steering sweep of *Hōkūleʻa*

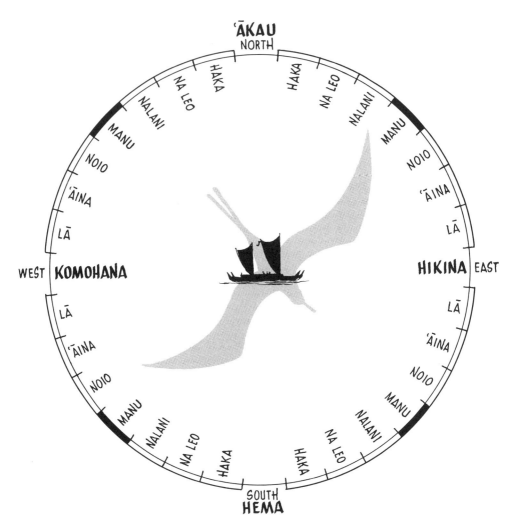

Nainoa's compass of 32 sectors

winds come from northeast and southeast. He might have used the established names of *hikina 'ākau* for northeast and *hikina hema* for southeast; *komohana hema* for southwest and *komohana 'ākau* for northwest. But he gave the quarter directions the name

Manu   "Bird," visualizing *Hōkūle'a* as a bird flying southeast, its head and neck outstretched and wings outspread.

Two more halvings gave thirty-two equal sectors, each of which he called a *house*. And to each he gave a Hawaiian name. Sectors east and west, where the sun rises and sets and where he expects the land to appear on the voyage, are the houses of

Lā   The place where *Lā*, the sun, rises and sets

ʻĀina   "The land," the direction in which the land is expected to be at the end of the voyage

Noio   Hawaiian name for the brown noddy tern that leads the wayfinder to the land.

The sky around the north and south polar regions is relatively devoid of stars. Nainoa's compass recognizes that darkness along with the importance of stars, dim and bright. In sectors north and south are the houses of

Haka   "Empty," denoting the emptiness and darkness of the region of the celestial poles

Nā Leo   "The voices," which, to Nainoa, are the "quiet voices of the stars"

Nalani   A name associated with Canopus, the second brightest star in the sky, and one that sets far to the southwest.

Since each quadrant is a mirror image of the adjacent quadrant, a prefix is needed to avoid ambiguity. For example, the winter sun rises in Noio. But there are four Noio, two in the east and two in the west. The Noio we want is *south* of east—Hema Hikina Noio. Since saying "Hema Hikina Noio" is awkward, we found it easier to use the English prefix, southeast, or SE, abbreviating it then to "SE Noio."

When the star compass disappears on cloudy nights, the wayfinder relies solely upon the surface of the sea.

Swells are long waves generated by pressure systems far beyond the horizon. Trade winds press on the surface of the sea and wrinkle it up into waves so big that they stretch from horizon to horizon and maintain orientation for days and weeks and months at a time.

The wayfinder checks the swell direction against the background of stars, sun, moon, planets. Mau uses five swells; they're always there for him. Nainoa seldom sees more than three. So sensitive is Mau to the motion of the ocean, because of his half-century's experience beside or on the sea, that he can actually be below deck and tell by the feel of the canoe if the steersman is performing his task adequately.

Wayfinding is continuous orientation, the wayfinder using all the available clues all the time. Nature provides clues, and the wayfinder integrates them into cognitive structures of compass and reference course. The picture created enables the navigator to know the way.

SOLVING A PROBLEM

Both Tahiti and Hawai'i lie within the tropics, between the "turning places of the sun." Reaching Tahiti from Hawai'i is a problem, for it lies upwind and upcurrent from Hawai'i. The canoe must cross two great west-flowing ocean currents.

Winds blow toward the equator from high pressure systems 30° each side of it. The spinning earth diverts the flow of air to the west, forming the northeast trade winds in the Northern Hemisphere and the southeast trade winds in the Southern.

Trade winds are low surface winds that travel over thousands of miles of fetch area at speeds of 15 to 20 knots. Toward the equator they weaken, and in the region of the Intertropical Convergence Zone (ITCZ) they are extremely weak. The ITCZ is the doldrums, a region noted for its dead calms and fluctuating winds, a region notorious for spawning cyclonic disturbances.

Moving westward like two gigantic rivers in the sea are the north equatorial and south equatorial ocean currents. Between them is the east-flowing equatorial countercurrent, a thin sheet of warm surface water washing back from the continent of Asia. Sporadic and shifting, the countercurrent, a thousand times wider than it is deep, contains big gyres and eddies and spin-offs from the north equatorial current.

Nainoa's reference course, his "map in mind," runs southeastward from Hawai'i and on into the doldrums. Then it bends directly south to cross the equator and meet the south equatorial current. It ends at Takapoto in the Tuamotus, not a destination but

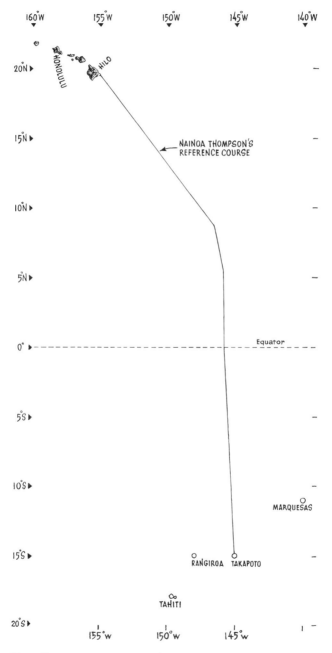

The reference course—a mental construct

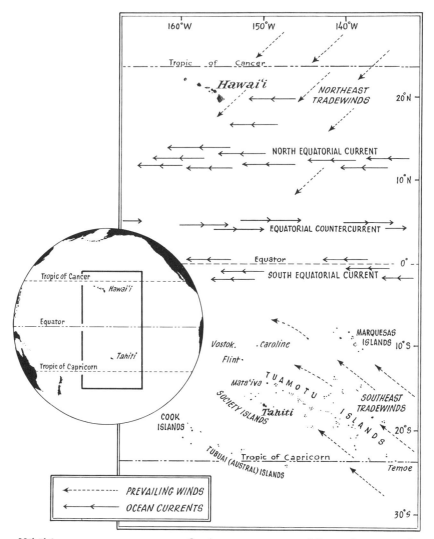

Hōkūleʻa must cross two great west-flowing ocean currents while moving eastward into two great trade wind systems to reach Tahiti.

a reference island. Built into Nainoa's reference course is an allowance for current. Should *Hōkūleʻa* spend an inordinate amount of time in a current, Nainoa would have to keep that in mind and make adjustments accordingly.

Wayfinding is a dead reckoning (from "ded"-uced) navigational system. The navigator knows where he starts and where he wants to go, and keeps track of speed and direction along the way. For Carolinian navigators, distance traveled is determined from an estimate of the speed of the canoe—from its sound and feel as it travels through the water and from the appearance of its wake.

The concept of speed, though, is of little meaning on the long Hawai'i-Tahiti route. Distance traveled is derived from a change in latitude. That comes from the stars.

Wayfinding requires windward landfall. In the absence of a way for determining longitude—and that does require instruments—the navigator sails to the windward side of the island he's looking for until he gets to the right latitude. Stars tell him that. Then downwind to the destination.

To reach Tahiti, "hold close to the wind," for Tahiti lies into the wind and current. The canoe must sail at least at right angles to the wind, "70° off the wind," if it has that capability.

In "holding close to the wind" on the Tahiti voyage, the *manu* (bow) of the canoe strikes the southeast swell head-on. The swell raises the bow and the canoe rocks back, then forward as the crest of the wave passes beneath the stern.

Ninety degrees from southeast is northeast. Trade winds from that direction generate a northeast swell that raises the port hull. It rides over the crest followed in quick snap-roll by the starboard hull. A combination of those two motions—pitch and roll—are clues to direction that the navigator uses in staying oriented when clouds hide the stars and make dark the sea.

But after a long voyage in the open ocean, how do you find the land when you know it's near? For the island is tiny and the sea is big.

Mau Piailug has pointed out that concentric circles of life surround every island—animals in the sea and animals in the air. Of greatest value to the wayfinder searching for land are the birds—land birds that go out to sea in the morning to feed and come back at night to sleep on the land. The diurnal flight patterns of such birds effectively increase the size of the island, a concept we call "expanded landfall."

Cloud patterns also expand the target. Often covering high islands are stationary clouds, quite different in appearance from the low,

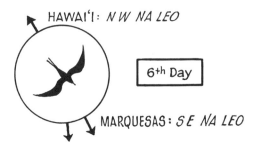

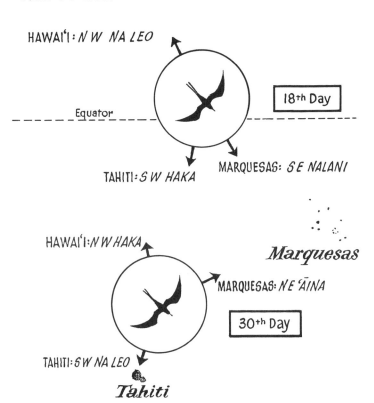

For Nainoa, the canoe is a bird, *manu*, flying toward Tahiti. Islands move through sectors of the star compass as the canoe moves southward. The Marquesas, for instance, move from SE Na Leo through SE Nalani and into NE 'Āina during the month's voyage.

Processing progress:
A hypothetical voyage of *Hōkūleʻa*

Hilo is the point of departure and the direction of the reference course is SE Manu.

Day 1. Course made good is SE Nalani, one house south of the reference line. At the end of this first day, the canoe is one house west of the reference line, one sailing day—100 miles—from Hilo.

Day 2. Course made good is SE Manu. At the end of the 2nd day, the canoe is one house west of the reference line and two sailing days—200 miles—from Hilo.

Day 3. Course made good, SE Noio. At the end of the 3rd day, the canoe is back on line and three sailing days—300 miles—from Hilo.

Day 4. Course made good, SE Noio. At the end of the 4th day, the canoe is one house east of the line and four sailing days—400 miles—from Hilo.

Day 5. Speed slows to half, and the direction shifts to SE Nalani/Na Leo. At the end of the 5th day, the canoe is on line, four and a half sailing days—450 miles—from Hilo.

Day 6. Again the canoe moves slowly in the direction of SE Nalani/Na Leo. At the end of the 6th day, the canoe is one house west of the line and five sailing days—500 miles—from Hilo.

rapidly moving trade wind clouds. A clue to low islands may be a green color of a lagoon reflecting up onto the underside of clouds. And in the water, currents and color are clues, also wave reflection and diffraction patterns.

So with a system and strategy worked out, Nainoa was ready for the sea. As in the 1976 voyage, the Polynesian Voyaging Society would require that an escort vessel accompany *Hōkūle'a* and maintain visual contact.

Ishka, a sloop belonging to Alex and Elsa Jakubenko, was chosen to be the escort. The escort would remain behind the canoe, continually varying its position relative to it so as not to interfere with the navigational experiment. A line-of-sight radio would enable the two vessels to communicate with each other. A single sideband radio would enable the escort vessel to communicate great distances, but the canoe would not have access to the outside world. Nor would they want it. The escort vessel was also charged with keeping track of position by means of celestial navigation, transmitting that information back to Honolulu—information, of course, that was not shared with the *Hōkūle'a*. A transponder aboard the canoe would enable *Ishka* to track the canoe in the event that the two vessels should become separated.

Hōkūle'a might have departed from Honolulu. Mau might have done it. But Nainoa wanted a departure point as far east as possible. He chose Hilo for that, the maximum initial easting assuring a greater probability of successful landfall. Getting to Hilo, though, turned out to be one of *Hōkūle'a*'s epic encounters with the sea.

In Peril on the Sea

*T*he 150-year old Kawaiahaʻo Church reverberates as the mighty organ plays the solid harmony and measured beat of the Mariner's Hymn.

"Eternal father, strong to save . . ."

Gordon Piʻianaiʻa, captain of the *Hōkūleʻa,* stands with his wife, Billie, and their two sons, Chad and Chris. He has prepared them for this voyage, the first stage of which begins tomorrow with *Hōkūleʻa*'s sailing from Honolulu to Hilo. Each time Gordon goes to sea, the family talks over the risks of ocean voyaging and the remote possiblity that he might never return.

"Whose arm doth bind the restless wave . . ."

Standing nearby is Mau Piailug. He is ready for the voyage, having prepared himself for it mentally by carving a model of his Satawal canoe. Next to Mau is Tava Taupu, a Marquesan from the island of Nuku Hiva. Tava began sailing even before he started walking, so the sea is no stranger to him.

"Who bidst the mighty ocean deep . . ."

Next to Tava is a member of the board of directors of the Polynesian Voyaging Society, Chuck Larson, a young man who already has had several exciting encounters with the sea. Beside him is Chad Baybayan, a carpenter-student from the island of Maui, destined to become intrigued with the art of wayfinding.

"Its own appointed limits keep . . ."

Behind them stand Jo-Anne Sterling and her husband, Leon. Together they made *Hōkūleʻa* a viable experience to thousands of school children as they sailed it among the islands of Hawaiʻi on an extended educational venture. Leon, head of the canoe committee, has seen to it that a new deck was lashed to *Hōkūleʻa* and that the canoe is in the finest shape. He has prepared himself for the sea by spending time alone in the mountains.

105

Kawaiaha'o churchyard

"Oh hear us when we cry to thee . . ."

Here in this church we are in touch with the kings and queens of Hawai'i who affirmed the monarchy and expressed a belief in God. Within these walls Kamehameha III spoke the beautiful words, now Hawaii's motto, *Ua mau ke ea o ka 'āina i ka pono,* "The life of the land is preserved in righteousness." And here William Charles Lunalilo walked down the aisle, thanking the people who had elected him supreme monarch of the land.

A sense of continuity of life pervades Kawaiaha'o. The church itself is made of organic materials. From the sea came coral for the walls, and from the mountains came the wood for the rafters and roof beams that bridge those coral walls.

With "patience and zeal" workers shaped the converging materials into straight, strong, rectangular form, broken only by the rounded tops of balcony windows. Where power is expressed in simplicity, this place is indeed most powerful.

The organ and voices swell into a mighty affirmation of power and supplication,

"For those in peril on the sea."

Next morning the crews of *Hōkūle'a* and the escort vessel, *Ishka,* meet at Pier 12 in downtown Honolulu for the first stage in a 6,000-mile ocean voyage—getting *Hōkūle'a* to Hilo, the point from which Nainoa has elected to depart. A month earlier we had gathered here for the rededication of the canoe, the Reverend Kealanahele then reminding us, "Whenever you are sailing *Hōkūle'a* another is always present—the spirit of Eddie Aikau."

"Cast off!" Lines slacken, and *Hōkūle'a* moves slowly away from the pier and into the channel. Standing by in the open sea is *Ishka,* constant companion of *Hōkūle'a* for the next four months. The hands of the Aloha Tower clock are straight up as *Hōkūle'a* meets the deep ocean swells and begins bobbing gently as wind fills its sails.

We feel alone. Yet behind the reflective facades of Honolulu highrises are thousands of people watching our progress. What's in a departure? Any departure? Particularly this one—a double-hulled voyaging canoe with golden crab-claw sails heading for a rendezvous with an angry sea?

Darkness is falling as we approach Moloka'i. For the next several hours the sweeping beam of ʻĪlio Point lighthouse will be with us. At midnight 4,000-foot sea cliffs are towering above us, invisible in this darkness. Aboard *Ishka* we're learning how truly difficult is the task of escorting—how startling it is suddenly to lose sight of *Hōkū-leʻa* when a rain squall casts its blackness between the two vessels.

Sunlight is touching the tops of Maui's two gigantic shield volcanoes as we begin crossing Pailolo Channel. Good winds are coming out of the north. But those winds gradually weaken as we move past the 650-foot volcanic cone, Kahakuloa Head, on Maui's northeastern side. At noon the winds stop.

To assure a reasonable arrival time in Hilo, *Ishka* takes *Hōkūleʻa* in tow. Most of the afternoon we spend in crossing the huge, open Kahului Bay where two centuries ago Hawaiians had greeted Captain Cook upon his return from Alaska in an unsuccessful search for the fabled Northwest Passage.

We are off Paʻuwela Point and over the northeast rift zone of Haleakalā as the sun sets behind Puʻu Kukui, the mile-high summit of the West Maui Mountains. During the night we are again moving along sea cliffs, this time those at the edge of Haleakalā where, between Honomanū and Nuaʻailua, the winding road to Hāna hangs 200-feet above the breaking waves. The Southern Cross is tilting toward the west and we're heading for Sagittarius rising as the sun comes up.

The ocean is smooth as we move past the black basaltic columns of Keʻākulikuli Point, now pink with living organisms. It's flat and glassy at Hāna-of-the-Low-Lying-Clouds where green meadows run upward and disappear into the clouds at 3,500 feet. Rough ʻAlenuihāhā Channel lies ahead.

A red cinder cone, 430-foot Kaʻuiki Head, marks the entrance to Hāna Bay. Waves have worn deeply into it, exposing its internal structure. A cave at its base is the birthplace of Kaʻahumanu, favorite wife of Kamehameha I. A bronze tablet marks that historic spot and reminds us of the marble plaque in the foyer of Kawaiahaʻo Church that recognizes the influence of this spirited woman:

Elisabeth Kaahumanu, daughter of Keeaumoku and Namahana. Born about 1773 at the foot of the hill Kauiki on East Maui; became a wife of Kamehameha I at 13. After the death of Kamehameha III in 1823 she wisely ruled the Hawaiian people as queen regent until her death in 1832.

Although naturally proud and haughty, she early in her regency humbly accepted Jesus as her Saviour.

Beyond Kaʻuiki lie the remains of an ancient Hawaiian temple platform, the Hale o Lono *heiau*. Nearby is the place where the demi-god Māui, after fashioning a magic fishhook and baiting it with the sacred *ʻalae* bird, paddled beyond the horizon to perform his heroic task of pulling the islands out of the sea. Māui's Fishhook (some call it Scorpius) is now in the sky for everyone on earth to see. We saw it this morning rising just ahead of the sun.

A little farther west is Ka Iwi o Pele, the cinder cone from which Lono-muku made his ascent into the sky to go and live on the moon. And in this quiet place we sail across a surprisingly sharp line that divides smooth shallow water from the deep, agitated water of ʻAlenuihāhā Channel that separates Maui from the island of Hawaiʻi, a channel notorious for its rough water. Soon *Ishka* is pitching and rolling in 10-foot seas with *Hōkūleʻa* following gracefully at the end of the tow line. The channel lies ahead; beyond that a passage along the Hāmākua coast of the island of Hawaiʻi, famous for its sea cliffs. With luck we'll be in Hilo tonight.

It is important for *Hōkūleʻa* to have an escort, and she is fortunate to have someone willing to do that difficult task. Alex Jakubenko commands this sturdy 48-foot sloop which he fashioned of steel. He also built the 60-foot *Meotai* that escorted *Hōkūleʻa* in 1976. Alex, the boat-builder, has a background as varied as it is cosmopolitan: Ukranian, Russian, French Underground, Australian, and soon American, as he and his wife Elsa are becoming citizens.

Elsa, the navigator, spends much of her time in the chart room plotting our position and tidying up *Ishka,* for this sloop is their home. Helping Alex at the wheel is John Eddy, a carpenter in his mid-twenties on his first long ocean trip. He's learning how *Ishka* responds to wind and wave and what to do to gain maximum sailing efficiency.

Good news on the weather; the northerlies are returning. However, that won't really happen until tomorrow afternoon and we'll already be in Hilo. Even now the wind is beginning to pick up; spray is drenching the *Hōkūleʻa* crew, all clad in brand-new foul-weather gear.

Telltales on *Ishka*'s shroud lines wave in the wind like green transparent fish. Swells are building to 12 feet as we reach the mid-point of ʻAlenuihāhā Channel, still fairly smooth. Behind us to the north is a long, thin streak of black cloud over Molokaʻi that is moving rapidly toward us. Above that ominous black line is a white mass bulging into an anvil-headed cloud at stratospheric altitude. We're fascinated at the sight, somewhat apprehensive, and little aware of the magnitude of the event it presages.

I push the buttons on the VHF radio. It beeps twice in seeking out the weather channel. Accompanying this menacing front are "locally heavy showers along the leading edge and for several hundred miles behind. Showers may produce locally strong and gusty winds." Sounds fairly benign.

Alex, with his sharp intuitive sense of the sea, wonders if it wouldn't be a good idea to head for the lee side of the island of Hawaiʻi to seek protection from the weather. But with Hilo only 30 miles dead ahead and with "locally gusty winds" following the front, we press on toward our destination.

Just before sunset it hits.

So sudden the fury of the storm! So violent the eruption of the sea! And so knowing Mau's comment, "More worse than typhoon!"

Fifty-knot, gale-force winds whip the sea into 20-foot waves, slashing spray horizontally. We watch *Hōkūleʻa* climbing up a big wave, twisting over its crest, then plunging downward into the trough of the upcoming mountain of water.

Another big wave approaches. *Ishka* rides up and over it. *Hōkūleʻa* is momentarily screened out as the taut tow line disappears under the wave. The wave starts breaking and John shouts, "It's going to eat the canoe this time!" Somehow, as usual, the wave works its way underneath the canoe and *Hōkūleʻa* nods reassuringly.

Tormented by the sea but tethered to *Ishka*, the canoe rides the tempest with dignity. Momentarily the tow line slackens. *Hōkūleʻa* runs over it, wrapping the line around the bow of the port hull. Freeing the line in this treacherous sea is a dangerous task, yet it is one that must be, and is, accomplished.

Wind and wave are driving us toward the rocky coast of Hāmākua. The stakes in this battle are clear and unambiguous. We either hold against the sea or crash onto the cliffs. Both vessels are in good shape; that's not the problem. The problem is our proximity to the land. Had this happened in the open sea we'd not be in trouble. But we *are* in trouble with the sea cliffs of Waipi'o so close.

The gray afternoon is darkening as we catch our last glimpse of *Hōkūle'a* still riding high in the water. We must keep heading into the wind. That's not easy, for the high hulls act as sails and the canoe goes broadside to the wind, sideways to the swells. Until we got both vessels turned into the wind, *Hōkūle'a* was traveling beside *Ishka, en echelon,* not behind it. *Ishka*'s engines are straining at 2,200 rpm. Alex checks them frequently to see that they are not over-heating.

How can any vessel stand this battering we've been enduring for the last hour? Amazing that the ancients came through seas like these. How could groups of canoes have stayed together in storm and darkness? Or did they?

The tow line is now disappearing into the blackness, but we know that *Hōkūle'a* is out there magnificently riding this crazy sea. Our technology allows us to "see" in the dark. I push the buttons on the VHF and while *Hōkūle'a* is responding I turn on the RDF (radio direction finder). A rotating beam of electrons sweeping the face of the cathode ray tube stops at 140 degrees. They're out there all right—right off our starboard quarter.

Frequently I call Honolulu Coast Guard Communication Station (COMSTA) to report our condition. "Honolulu COMSTA, this is Whiskey Hotel Alpha 9072, the *Ishka*. We're now turned into the wind and into the sea, holding a position about 10 miles off Waipi'o."

We're one vessel with two captains and a common fate. Alex commands the bow, Gordon commands the stern. The deck between is 500 feet of ⁵⁄₈-inch tow line, now thinned to ³⁄₈ inch by the stresses and strains of the stormy sea. Alex is determined; "We're one boat, one people."

Two hours of battling. No respite. It is prudent to ask Coast Guard for assistance—assistance, not rescue. Two forces are in balance: the wind pushing us toward the cliffs and the engine keeping us where we are. Equilibrium is bound to shift. Assistance will make certain that it shifts in our favor.

"*Ishka,* this is COMSTA. Understand you are maintaining your position 10 miles off Waipi'o, not making headway, not losing. Is that correct? Over."

"COMSTA, this is *Ishka*. Roger. We are maintaining. We can maintain only if the tow line remains intact. We cannot be sure. That's why we're asking for assistance."

"*Ishka*, COMSTA. Roger. Understand. Stand by for phone patch to Honolulu Rescue."

"Roger, *Ishka* standing by."

Rescue! Honolulu *Rescue?* Little did we realize when we sang the Mariner's Hymn at Kawaiahaʻo Church last Sunday that on Wednesday we would be the ones in peril on the sea. Rescue. The word conjures up in my mind paintings by artists depicting tumultuous seas with spume blowing like sand against vessels about to be dashed upon the shore. Now we're the ones in that picture with a fate not yet determined. How innocent the voyage, how cruel the fate!

Honolulu Rescue is also having its problems tonight. Several vessels are in trouble and need help. Two are now sinking.

"*Ishka*, this is Honolulu Rescue. What is the condition of the personnel aboard *Hōkūleʻa?*"

Gordon reports: "We're sitting here with our life jackets on. Man-overboard pole and lights are on deck. Safety lines are rigged and safety harnesses are fastened. We're ready. We plan to stay with the canoe, but if we get in too close to the shore there's nothing we can do."

A big wave smashes into us. In a moment it will catch *Hōkūleʻa*. Gordon stops transmitting and we hear a crackling. Then he comes back, "A big wave just smashed over us. Sea anchors are ready and waiting to be deployed, whatever help they may be in this wind and ocean."

Alex takes the microphone and talks to Gordon. "Hopefully we can both come around. So don't worry, sir. We have a 50-50 chance of making it. I shall try my best. If you can do your best, we can do it, too. So don't worry. Chin up! Chin up, sir!"

"Okay Alex," comes back Gordon's weary drawl in this third hour of battle. "We'll just hang on."

"*Ishka*, this is Honolulu Rescue. If your situation deteriorates do you think you'll have any trouble in rescuing the personnel of *Hōkūleʻa?* Over."

Rescue? Trouble rescuing? Rescuing in this heavy sea and darkness? "Honolulu Rescue, this is *Ishka*. Difficult to say. We've never tried it before."

Shroud lines whistle in the wind as *Ishka* wallows in the sea. We're not far from land. Two bewildered birds land on the spreader arms of *Ishka*'s mast seeking a moment's respite from the gale. Then they disappear. We hope they find land. We hope we do not.

Radio transmission from one of the sinking vessels is becoming more and more broken. Then silence. We wonder the fate of that crew. And wonder the fate of ours.

"Hōkūleʻa. Ishka."

"Yah," replies Gordon. In this fourth hour of our ordeal standard radio operating procedure is becoming abbreviated.

"We're bringing it around a little more into the wind," says Alex, "a little more into the wind, sir."

"Okay, Alex, we'll see how that works."

Where are we? Perilously close. Rain ceases for a while and we're able to see a few lights along the shore. Alex goes down to the cabin to study the chart of lighthouses.

"Come, have a look!" The cabin is pitch dark except for the illuminated display of numbers on the VHF and for the flashlight he's using. I grasp the handrails overhead and crawl, crabwise, hand-over-hand to keep from being thrown against the bulkheads.

Alex shines the flashlight on the chart. *Ishka* takes a big wave, rolls 45 degrees, and we hang onto the chart table. "I think we're here . . . between this light . . . and that one. See . . . because this one is here . . . and that one is there. . . . So we must be here. Right?"

We go topside to check, then return to the chart room. "Of course! We're looking at this one . . . right here . . . and that's that one . . . right there. Yes, we must be right here. Good!"

I call over that good news to *Hōkūleʻa*. "Alex thinks we now have an 80 percent chance of making it." That's a real turning point in their fate—from 50 to 80 percent, and we all relax a bit.

"Whiskey Hotel Alpha 9072, the *Ishka*, this is Honolulu COMSTA. Understand you are 10 miles off Waipiʻo and holding. Is that correct? Over."

A different voice, perhaps a change of watch. How comforting to know that someone is closely watching us! Few if any other countries take as good care of those at sea as does the United States with its Coast Guard.

COMSTA wants an update. Now in our fifth hour in the tempest it's my tired voice that responds, "We think we're a little north of Waipi'o. Hard to tell in this storm. We're not in trouble. Holding. We do not need rescue but we do need assistance." Then I add, "We hope this weather clears."

Amidst the efficient formality of cryptic radio procedure comes back a surprisingly warm reply, "We hope so, too!"

Honolulu Rescue talks to the crew of a vessel now sinking off the coast of Lāna'i. A Coast Guard cutter is on the scene but they've not yet seen the vessel. An airplane with powerful strobe lights is circling but they've not spotted it. And their watersoaked flares are inoperable. Honolulu Rescue begins coaching the crew on the proper procedure for stepping into the dark sea.

Gordon, Leon, Jo-Anne, Tava, Mau, Chuck, and Chad huddle close to the VHF on *Hōkūle'a* to hear what's going on in the outside world. They wait. That's all they can do, wait and hope. I relay them messages. Anything—anything to keep in contact—world news, conditions of other vessels, precautionary advice, weather reports, incongruities: "Waterspouts may accompany this frontal system. Caution is advised. If you see one, avoid it. If you cannot, lie down on the ground and cover your head."

No one is more acutely aware of the rocky Hāmākua coast than the seven aboard *Hōkūle'a*. So with nothing to do but wait, I proceed to describe the geology of the region which, in this darkness, they neither see nor care to see.

"Behind you is the Kohala volcanic shield. It's a region of magnificent waterfalls, towering sea cliffs, and hazardous trails. The shield, rising a mile above sea level, is made of countless flows of thin-bedded primitive olivine basalts with porphyries at the surface. The great flat-floored valleys of Waipi'o and Pololū were carved out of the shield during the past million years."

The radio direction finder shows Haleakalā to be dead ahead. We're doing fine. "Ninety percent sure," says jubilant Alex in this sixth hour of the storm. I relay the message, adding with a bit of whimsy, "And I can think of no more beautiful place in this world to end up on than the rocky Hāmākua coast of Hawai'i, the birthplace of Kamehameha I."

Suddenly aboard *Ishka* we hear a loud crack. A jolt. A jerk. We all know what has happened. "The tow line has snapped!" screams Alex against the raging sea.

The dream is gone. Shattered. *Hōkūleʻa* is about to be dashed to pieces on the Hāmākua cliffs. The Polynesian Voyaging Society cannot live through this failure. The navigation project is ended. The canoe is finished and our task is to rescue the seven.

"Honolulu COMSTA, this is *Ishka*. The tow line has broken. *Hōkūleʻa* is adrift and heading for the Waipiʻo cliffs."

"*Ishka*, this is COMSTA. Roger. Understand. *Hōkūleʻa* is adrift. Proceed to evacuate the crew at your own discretion."

I call Gordon. "We've just informed COMSTA of the broken tow line. We're standing by for the rescue operation."

"Rescue?" asks Gordon. "What for? The tow line's okay."

Okay? How could it be? We check. He's right. It's intact—thin but still intact.

"Honolulu COMSTA, this is *Ishka*. The tow line is intact. *Hōkūleʻa* is with us yet and not adrift as we had reported. Something has happened to *Ishka* that we cannot explain."

"*Ishka*, COMSTA. Did you sustain hull damage?"

"Honolulu COMSTA, this is *Ishka*. We don't know. Nothing obvious. The steering is different. We hear a sloshing sound down below. Engines are working fine and the stuffing box is okay."

We continue uneasily on our way, listening, checking, wondering. We're mystified by the force of the impact (if that's what it was), the strange sounds down below, and the unusual movement of the sloop.

"*Ishka*, this is *Cape Newagen*."

A woman's voice! That's Lieutenant Beverly Kelley! She's the first woman ever to command a Coast Guard cutter in the Pacific. "Request you turn on a strobe light." They're close. How quickly they got here! Not long ago they were helping in that Lānaʻi rescue and now they're with us. John rigs a strobe light to flash against the sail.

"*Ishka*, this is *Cape Newagen*. Do you see a blue rotating light?" They must have spotted us. They're close, really close. I relay the message topside and John hollers, "We've got it! We've got it! A beautiful blue!"

I report to the cutter, "*Cape Newcastle*, this is *Ishka*." Newcastle? Did I say Newcastle? I'm so tired and relieved that it doesn't seem to matter. But *Cape Newagen* is having trouble with the name *Hōkūleʻa*, calling it "Hukilau." "Are all persons aboard the *Hukilau* okay?" The names are troubling but the feeling is so right at this one-in-the-morning hour after a seven-hour encounter with the sea.

"*Ishka*, can you handle a 1½-inch tow line?"

"Yes, it's a matter of maneuvering into position."

"What is the hull speed of *Hōkūle'a?*" A line of questioning continues to gather information upon which to base good decisions.

"You seem to be towing fine now," says *Cape Newagen* after observing us for several minutes. "Seas are diminishing. Suggest you proceed on your own. We'll stand by for an hour until you get around the point. Do you think that you can then make it to a port on the lee side of Hawai'i?"

We three—*Cape Newagen*, *Hōkūle'a*, and *Ishka*—travel together around 'Upolu Point and into the calmer waters on the lee side of the Big Island. An hour later we bid aloha to the cutter as it peels off and heads back to Mā'alaea, Maui, continually monitoring us as we proceed southward along the coast to Kawaihae.

Stars are beginning to fade. Here the waters are flat and the coast is misty. The sun is rising behind Mauna Kea as we enter the harbor at Kawaihae beside the huge Pu'ukoholā *heiau* of Kamehameha. We secure the canoe and give our accounts to the radio, newspaper, and TV reporters who have been waiting for us. We're happy to see them but tired after having completed a crucial part of what on Sunday the Reverend Abraham Akaka had called, "The Great Adventure."

We're celebrating our arrival in a most appropriate manner when Leon Sterling, square-jawed, bald, and powerful, gently picks me up for having pushed him into a TV interview, and, allowing me time to take the wallet out of my pocket, jumps with me into the sea. How good to feel the coolness of the water, to swim back and forth from bow to stern beneath the high deck of the canoe, to look up at those tight lashings and know what a rugged vessel it really is!

Something happened. The trip, a near tragedy, brought the crew together in mutual respect for excellent seamanship in dealing with peril on the sea on a venture "more worse than typhoon."

What was it that went thump in the night?

We'll never know.

Waiting for the Wind

We walk across the bridge to Coconut Island in Hilo Lagoon for *Hōkūle'a*'s departure ceremony. It is Sunday, March 9, 1980. Five years ago yesterday the canoe was launched. Since then it has made one round trip to Tahiti, attempted another, and tested Kealaikahiki as a possible path to Tahiti. Today's ceremony consecrates it to the task of furthering our knowledge of wayfinding.

A rectangular arrangement of mats beneath palm trees is the ceremonial center. Seated on a mat behind the large, wooden 'awa bowl is Captain Gordon Pi'ianai'a. Sitting at his right is first mate Leon Sterling. At Gordon's left is Nainoa Thompson. About 500 yards beyond them, across the lagoon, is *Hōkūle'a* bobbing gently at its mooring in front of the Naniloa Hotel. Seated at the place of honor opposite the trio of officers are Mau Piailug and Myron "Pinky" Thompson, who is head of the steering committee and Nainoa's father. Facing each other across the long sides of the rectangle are the "down" and "up" crews.

The mellow sounding of the conch shell announces the beginning of the ceremony. Crew member Sam Ka'ai officiates, declaring this ceremonial site now to be a spiritual place. Covering Sam's shoulders is a short cloak of *ki* leaves. On his head is a lei of forest fern, *palapalai*. George Haope, clad in a long, pure white ceremonial robe, is an ancient spirit as he moves about chanting a Hawaiian blessing.

Strong gusty winds are coming out of the east bringing intermittent rain. "Rain is a good omen," says Israel Kamoku, pastor of Ho'omanu Na'auao Church in Pāpa'ikou, offering a prayer. A vision has revealed to him that the first 200 miles of the journey will be rough. After that it will be fast and smooth.

Sam performs the 'awa ceremony. Dipping a coconut shell into

117

Sam Ka'ai

the bowl, he offers the bitter brew to each member of the crew. Each, in turn, drinks from this "vessel of the family of the canoe," *Ipu o 'Ohana o Wa'a,* signifying unity.

The ceremony is a melding with ancient ways, reawakening within each of us a feeling for the past. Reaffirmed in ritual is *'ohana,* a concept of family that governed a people long ago.

Sam presents Mau with a single whale-tooth pendant which he has worn since the 1976 voyage. Then he places two *lei huluhulu* (feather leis) on the ground before Gordon, Leon, and Nainoa. Later the leis, traditional wind indicators, will be tied to the canoe's masts.

Nainoa rises and goes to Mau Piailug. "It was you who inspired us and gave us strength. You live the sea. We do not. We are your children." Young and intense, tears fill his eyes, yet he speaks without hesitation. "Now is our time to learn. We must sail or forever be silent."

Sam blesses two human-like images that he has carved from *māmane* wood. *Kāne o Hōkūle'a,* the male figure, is the "chief article." The female figure, *Wahine o Mo'o o Malu'uluolele* is the "chief witness," symbolizing witness to the ceremony and the journey.

A canoe carries the images across the lagoon and they are tied, one to each *manu*, or finlike stern, of *Hōkūle'a*. The *lei huluhulu* are then fastened to the top of each mast. Again the conch shell sounds, terminating the ceremony and carrying a message: "We may have to wait for the wind, but spiritually we are already on our way."

Ceremonially separated from the land and symbolically committed to the sea, the crew in ancient times would remain quietly apart from the rest of the community to wait for the right conditions. Today, though, we walk together back over the bridge and to the hotel. Families and friends linger, hoping to see a departure but knowing that it cannot be today; so they return to Honolulu.

Monday morning. The sea is gray and rough. Strong winds are still blowing from the east. Nainoa has gone back to O'ahu to "look at the weather." That's where his experience in weather prediction has been. Trying to judge the weather from Hilo is difficult for him; the conditions are different here, with clouds pressing against the base of the high mountains, Mauna Kea and Mauna Loa.

The crew is housed on the fifth floor of the Hilo Hawaiian Hotel. It's a pleasant suite of rooms which, with lovable whimsy, we call "the barracks." We have a view of the gentle green slopes sweeping up to the snows of Mauna Kea and downslope to the villages of Pāpa'ikou and Pepe'ekeo. Quiet Hilo lies at the corner of L-shaped Hilo Bay. Only rarely is the town's serenity broken by flows of lava from Mauna Loa and by earthquake-generated waves funneling into Hilo Bay.

Roy Benham, a distinguished white-haired man of Hawaiian ancestry, is in charge of provisioning *Hōkūle'a* and feeding the crew in both Hilo and Tahiti. He's a good manager, dealing easily with the unpredictable, never knowing how many persons will show up for meals as crew and visitors drift casually in and out. Somehow there's always plenty on the table.

Hilo hospitality is warm. Family of the crew and friends bring food, and the Dante Carpenters invite us to a *lū'au*. We are not at all separated from the community as was the custom in ancient times. Instead, we have cars that whisk us into town on mindless shopping sprees for things we don't need, as well as a telephone and television to keep us continually in touch with what's going on in the outside world. We're not alone.

Tuesday morning. Mau, Chad, Pat, Buddy, Leon, and I leave the hotel at 4:30 A.M. to watch the dawning of the day. Nainoa is doing the same on Oʻahu. We drive south and east from Hilo to get out from under the low-lying clouds so that we can see the conditions far out to sea. Mau, his elbows on the dashboard of the van, is looking up at the sky as we speed along the highway in Puna, through dark fields of orchid and papaya.

"More farther," he says. We curve through the village of Pāhoa with its wooden buildings and board walks, then out onto the recent lava flows along the east rift of Kīlauea volcano.

"Stop!"

We get out of the van beside Puʻulena Crater and gather around Mau as the sky begins to lighten beyond Kapoho Crater and the distant Cape Kumukahi. Mau looks for "smoke" beneath the clouds, for subtleties that will assure favorable winds and send us on our way. Overhead is a hazy Third Quarter Moon that will be with us all morning.

Ten minutes of silence. Suddenly Mau bursts forth with, "Weather come good tomorrow. No more clouds. Wind come more north. Tomorrow all good!"

Sunrise reveals cinder cones and lava flows surrounding us. It's a desolate place. We are right on the rift zone of the world's most consistently active volcano. Red and brown cinder cones studding this forlorn region are interlaced with fantastic flows of jagged *ʻaʻā* and glistening *pāhoehoe*. We are standing over one of this planet's "hot spots." Leon tells Mau in animated pidgin what happened here, how it was that in 1960 lava flooded over Warm Springs and buried a favorite spa of ancient Hawaiian chiefs.

"Tomorrow, not today."

Back through the village of Pāhoa we travel and tuck under rain clouds ringing the mountains. We lapse into silence, each in his own world of excitement, listening to the sound of tires slapping on a wet pavement.

"Tomorrow weather come good."

All morning long we sit in the "barracks" talking of the weather until we have nothing more to say. Nainoa calls: "Winds are easterly and dying down. Tomorrow they'll probably be more northerly." Not much different from Mau's prediction. Nainoa has a difficult decision to make—when to commit to the sea. Just how does one keep personal excitement from intruding into good judgment?

Today, the 11th of March, is Nainoa's 27th birthday. We sing him a happy birthday song over the telephone and wish him well. Then we spend the rest of the day waiting for the wind.

Wednesday morning. Again we drive out from under hovering clouds, travel through the village of Pāhoa, and out onto the east rift.

Mau is right. Winds have shifted slightly to the north. Still it's overcast and not a very pleasant day. Neither is it all bad. Mau could sail in such weather, for he has had a lifetime of experience with the sea. Not Nainoa.

"Okay," says Mau. "We go."

Go? To Tahiti today? No; that decision is—and must be—Nainoa's. Mau simply means that there's no point in watching any longer, for the weather is the same as it was yesterday. He knows that Nainoa there on Oʻahu will be cautious.

Back through forests of ʻōhiʻa and *kamani* we go, once again through the quiet village of Pāhoa now coming alive, then underneath the clouds pushing against the mid-slopes of those two largest volcanoes on this planet.

Another day of watching and waiting. Some crew members go fishing; others go into town. Nobody stays away for long. We can't. We're trapped by weather that might change, and bound together by a loyalty that will not change.

Four-thirty Thursday morning. East winds and overcast. Same as yesterday. Same as the day before. Same as the day before that. No point in looking for the wind today. Instead we spend the day in the "barracks" enjoying Roy Benham's breakfast, lunch, and dinner.

Pat Aiu plays slack-key guitar. Harry Ho strums an ʻukulele and Buddy McGuire sings in falsetto. Marion Lyman-Mersereau and John Eddy sit on the floor splitting *ki* leaves for head leis that Roy is making for the farewell—whenever that might be. Mike Tongg sits in a corner playing a solitary game of *kapu*. Henry Piailug manages the telephone and makes frequent calls to the weather service in Hilo for the marine forecast. Elsa Jakubenko and Lee Kyselka sit in the middle of the room talking and working with *ki* leaves as Steve Somsen smiles and checks the list of supplies yet to be loaded. Media people call or drop by to see us. But there's no story. Not yet.

Chinese fortune cookies provide pleasant diversion. "Finish that half-done project; the time is right." Another says, "You'll be stuck with a boring conversation, probably with that turkey on your left." Quick glances and smiles follow that one. "The more you say the less people remember." How apropos of the ennui we're experiencing! Steve adds redundant profundity to the going-nowhere theme with, "No matter where you are, there you are."

We sense a change but nothing is different. Even though small-craft warnings are still up and visibility is decreasing, something seems to be happening. Rain clouds move in and hide Pepeʻekeo Point, then Pāpaʻikou, and at mid-morning the breakwater, much closer to us, is gone. Henry calls the marine weather forecaster to find that "winds are from the east at 25 knots with seas at 12 feet; 40 knots in channels with 20-foot seas." How comfortable the hotel! At noon the sun once again appears and the familiar landmarks are restored. "Get ready to husk coconuts," says Gordon. "We have to do it soon before the red ants take over."

Something's in the air. We feel it, though nothing is obvious. Nainoa calls. Last night he visited with Eddie Aikau's family who sent their blessing and wanted the crew to know of their solid support of this *Hōkūleʻa* venture.

"The weather will tell us when to go," says Nainoa with remarkable restraint. "We'll just wait."

Friday morning. For the first time in five days we see the top of Mauna Kea, the mountain so profoundly symbolic in Nainoa's thinking. We stop at Weather Service and find that the total picture is still not good. Two fronts are out there, stationary, and diverting normal trade wind flow from northeast to east. The system hasn't moved in two weeks. No wonder there's been no change.

Nainoa appears at noon: "Tomorrow we'll go if it's no worse than this. Conditions are not ideal, but adequate."

The crew gathers that evening in a special room for final instructions. In an atmosphere of restrained excitement Nainoa talks in quiet tones of his navigational plan, now revised because of the weather. Originally he had wanted to sail straight east from Hilo for two days before turning south. Present conditions will not allow that. "Winds will determine the direction and I'll have to make up for deviations along the way."

With the weather somewhat promising and with our confidence in Nainoa, we're ready to go tomorrow. This is our last night on shore and we go to hear the Inkspots.

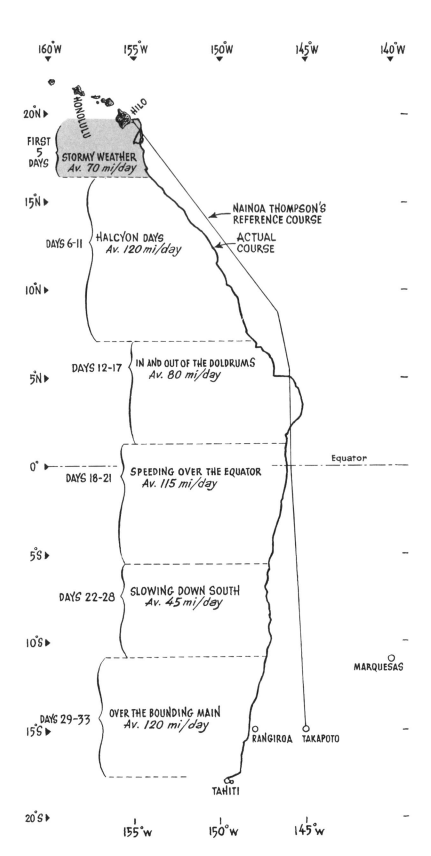

Stormy Weather

*I*t's a gray and gloomy Saturday morning, March 15, 1980. All over the island chain it is cloudy and rainy. Raining, raining—from South Point to Midway it is raining.

But rain is not our problem.

Our problem is the wind. For the past two weeks it has been blowing right out of the east—the worst of all possible winds for a Tahiti departure. But even though they're not ideal, they are "adequate." We're going.

Hōkūleʻa bobs gently at its mooring in front of the Naniloa Hotel. Huddled on the pier beneath black, tilted-back umbrellas is a group of friends and well-wishers. A spritely contrast in this somber, yet exciting scene is the crew of *Hōkūleʻa*. They're attired in brilliant yellow foul-weather gear as they move about the deck attending to their duties.

A prayer, a blessing, and the joining of hands. Warm tears mix with raindrops as we sing "Hawaiʻi Aloha." The circle expands and breaks, and once more a double-hulled voyaging canoe moves toward Tahiti.

"Honolulu COMSTA, this is Whiskey Hotel Alpha 9072, the *Ishka*. Reporting *Hōkūleʻa* underway at 1020."

Hōkūleʻa uses its 40-horsepower outboard engine to power across the relatively calm waters of Hilo Harbor. But as the canoe is clearing the breakwater, big ocean swells swamp the engine. It sputters and dies. *Ishka* passes a tow line to the canoe. For the next six hours we proceed in tandem, straight into the wind to assure clearance of Cape Kumukahi.

Seas are not high, 4 feet. Winds are not strong, 15 knots. But each vessel has an uneasy motion. I'm beginning to feel quite warm as I watch *Hōkūle'a* wallowing in the sea behind us. I blink and shake my head. Stand up to catch the cooling breeze. Strange. I can't quite believe what I think might be happening. A lightness . . . a slow swirling . . . a tilting sea . . . I lie down and let the warm rain fall on my face. *Ishka* pitches into waves, scoops up water that runs down the narrow deck, sloshes over me, and disappears out the scuppers.

Most of the next day and a half I'm in the forward bunk immersed in a world of sound and movement. *Ishka* creaks as it rolls. Halyards slap at the masts and strange chafing noises persist, like the sound of someone cutting heavy paper with scissors. Once in a while I go topside for a look and quickly return to collapse on the bunk. I think of almost nothing but getting an airplane here to pick me up. Otherwise, I'll get dehydrated, I'll go into shock, and they'll have to bury me here at sea not far from Hilo.

Few, if any, on either vessel are without discomfort. Only three persons appear on the deck of *Hōkūle'a,* stalwart ones who keep it sailing. After a few hours of towing and we're clear of Cape Kumu-kahi, the tow line is released and each vessel is on its own.

Steve Somsen, the on-board *Hōkūle'a* documenter, has no problem: "As I lie at rest in the compartment I share with Tava Taupu in port number 3, the canoe is still under tow. The constant motor sound from *Ishka* is heard, and there's a light patter of rain on the canvas spray shield. The water splashing around on the inside of the hull can also be easily heard. The compartment itself provides reasonable shelter that is relatively dry."

Each day Steve interviews Nainoa, the first interview beginning at sunset, 15 miles off Kalapana.

Steve: Where are we?
Nainoa: In the middle of the gray, man. I don't know.
Steve: Our course?
Nainoa: We're pointing a little higher than Hema Hikina Manu [SE Manu].
Steve: And the swells?
Nainoa: One from NE Manu hitting us broadside. Another from Hikina. Not many clues out here.
Steve: Why are we triced [the sails closed]?

Nainoa: When squalls come the wind's too strong.
Steve: And what's that do, drive us too far to the leeward?
Nainoa: No. Breaks the rigging.

Midnight, and we're east of Ka Lae (South Point), the most southerly place in the United States. We're 60 miles from Hilo—good progress for a half-day's sailing under difficult conditions. Frustration, though, lies ahead, and in two days we'll be back here, right where we are now.

Sunrise at the beginning of our second day finds us beneath a thick cloud blanket and moving straight south at a speed of 4 knots. Nainoa has only the surface of the sea for a clue to direction, no sun. We're 70 miles from Hilo and 70 from South Point and in no danger, but winds are becoming more easterly and we're in for a time of worsening conditions.

The weather report offers no solace: "Gale warnings are in effect for all Hawaiian waters and within 500 miles of the islands. Seas are 12 to 18 feet; winds are easterly 25 to 30 knots." *Hōkūle'a* estimates an even stronger wind of 35 knots gusting to 40 all afternoon.

Steve calls us on the VHF: "We're running bare-pole [the boom and gaff are down and only the mast remains]. Both Laehu [forward] and Lahope [aft] sails are lashed on deck. Sea anchors are streamed off the bow to slow our drift. The canoe is riding broadside to the wind. Considering the conditions, the ride is fairly comfortable."

Ishka tunnels through a wave and plops into a trough with tremendous thudding. Was that an island we hit or the bottom of the sea? A sturdy vessel this, that it can withstand all this pounding, and how sturdy the double-hulled canoe!

Ishka's mainsail blows out. Repairing it is a tedious task. Alex and the canvas fill the galley. He sits on the sail, bracing his feet against the other side of the galley to steady himself. For hours he works on the sail, diligently using a bosun's mitt to push a heavy needle through a double-thick canvas patch.

Mike Stroup has trouble using a knife. It slips, slitting his shin. He does his own first aid, bravely taking care of his injury. A doctor, Pat Aiu, is close by on the *Hōkūle'a*. That's comforting, but Mike does not think it necessary to call for his services.

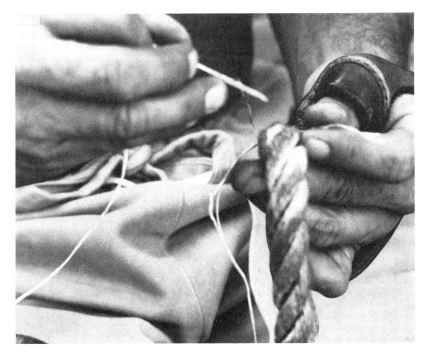

All afternoon and night *Hōkūleʻa* drifts rapidly westward in gale force winds. The night is dark, for clouds completely cover the sky. Even if clouds were not there it would still be dark, for this is the night of the New Moon. A whole month of moon phases lies yet ahead. The First Quarter Moon will find *Hōkūleʻa* with a broken boom. A Full Moon will light our way through the doldrums, and the Last Quarter will see our slowest night. Greeting us in Tahiti will be the next invisible New Moon.

Hōkūleʻa raises both sails at sunrise on the third day. Thirty miles of westward drift stops and the canoe moves southward.

Where are we? In a sense it doesn't matter, for we're nowhere near land. Still we'd like to know. Aboard *Ishka* we place a point on Chart 526 to represent where we think we are, an estimate based on our rate of drift. Aboard *Hōkūleʻa* Nainoa has no chart, only his mind. He assesses wind speed, the rate and direction of drift, and keeps it all in his head.

Ebullient Steve expresses a change in mood from dreary drift to active sailing on this 17th day of March:

St. Patrick's Day brings us a fresh breeze but still there's a fair amount of rain from time to time. Two blue-masked boobies are flying in tandem around the canoe. They've been escorting us for some time and they seem to be fascinated with the long feather telltale at the top of the Laehu sail. Three fishing lines are strung. Mau and Buddy are using steel hooks. Sam is using one made from bone. Several bags of coconuts are around the deck along with bunches of green bananas and a few papayas—gifts from Hilo friends.

The southward sprint is short-lived with a mid-morning squall approaching. *Hōkūle'a* drops both sails, and we notify Honolulu COMSTA: "*Hōkūle'a* is in a hove-to condition with sea anchors deployed. Request Coast Guard weather report." We give them our local observations. They, in turn, feed our report into a computer that integrates it with other observations and consults a weather satellite photo. Back comes a local forecast that leaves little to look forward to in terms of better weather.

"I think we're about 175 miles south of Hilo," says Nainoa (actually closer to 100). "It's difficult to keep track of speed and direction in this wind. Sometimes we go with one sail, then with two. Sometimes the sails are triced and sometimes they're down. Stars have not appeared to give us direction. Not even the sun. I'm starting the course right now, adding a lot of westerly deviation—eight houses to the west."

At noon we're straight south of Hilo, straight south of where we started and not far from the turn-around point on the 1977 Kealaikahiki trip. Nainoa is concerned about our westward drift. Winds have swung around so that they are not coming from the east. He knows that we can gain easting if we tack to the north. *Ishka* receives a message: "For the next six hours we'll be on a starboard tack" (the wind coming across the starboard hull). Under a gray sky we swing around and head back toward Cape Kumukahi, apparently doomed forever to wander this lonely tropic sea.

Alex spends another day on the floor of the galley patching the mainsail. His eyes are red from hours of strain; his fingers sore from the pressure of the needle and abrasion of the canvas. Lee and John lend a hand. Adding to the difficulty of making the repair is the increased rocking and bouncing we're experiencing on this starboard tack.

Leon Sterling, Jo-Anne Sterling, Harry Ho

Strobe lights are rigged at evening twilight. Jupiter, Saturn, and a few stars appear briefly in an opening in the clouds. Not for long, though, but long enough to raise the hope of better weather.

All night *Ishka*'s engines turn at full speed as we move into the wind and keep pace with *Hōkūle'a*. At times we travel smoothly, then we gently rock. Sometimes we cut through a wave and expect to fall into a trench. Instead, we do a roll and are thrown from side to side. A combination of wind and engine roar generates a sound like that of boxcars colliding and creates an impression of speed much greater than the 4 knots we're making.

Hōkūle'a's 4th day at sea begins as streaks of dawn touch the eastern horizon. Last night we gained 25 miles of easting, and now we're where we were at sunset on our first day. After the morning change of watch, we leave our starboard tack to begin a port tack that will last a month. We're safe and sound and hopeful that this will be a day of good progress.

Steve: How far from the reference line are we?
Nainoa: Not too far, maybe two houses west.

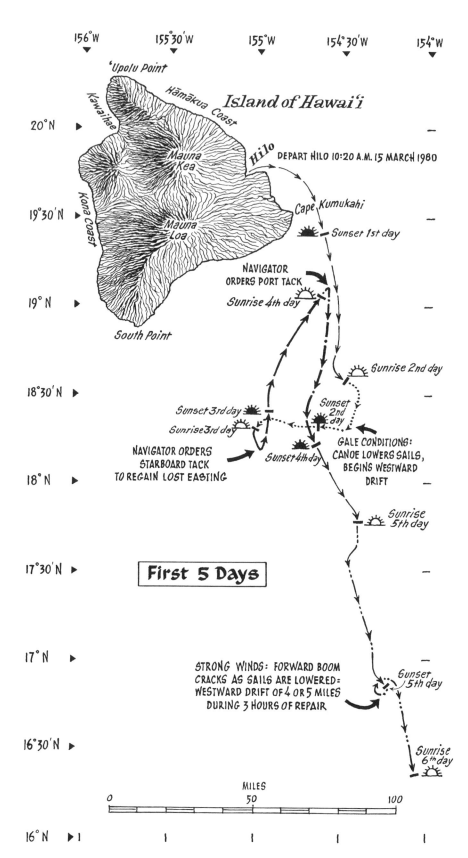

First 5 Days

156°W   155°30'W   155°W   154°30'W   154°W

'Upolu Point

Kawaihae

Hāmākua Coast

Island of Hawai'i

20°N

Mauna Kea

Hilo

DEPART HILO 10:20 A.M. 15 MARCH 1980

Kona Coast

19°30'N

Cape Kumukahi

Mauna Loa

Sunset 1st day

NAVIGATOR ORDERS PORT TACK

19°N

Sunrise 4th day

South Point

Sunrise 2nd day

18°30'N

Sunset 3rd day

Sunset 2nd day

Sunrise 3rd day

NAVIGATOR ORDERS STARBOARD TACK TO REGAIN LOST EASTING

Sunset 4th day

GALE CONDITIONS: CANOE LOWERS SAILS, BEGINS WESTWARD DRIFT

18°N

Sunrise 5th day

17°30'N

17°N

STRONG WINDS: FORWARD BOOM CRACKS AS SAILS ARE LOWERED: WESTWARD DRIFT OF 4 OR 5 MILES DURING 3 HOURS OF REPAIR

Sunset 5th day

16°30'N

Sunrise 6th day

MILES

0   50   100

16°N

Steve: How far from Hilo?

Nainoa: A little less than one sailing day.

Steve: And the swells?

Nainoa: The NE Manu swell is getting smaller and SE Manu bigger. But the biggest of all is coming right out of the east.

Steve: The wind?

Nainoa: It's a really lousy wind. We're just playing around out here doing nothing. We're trying to tack from here to Tahiti, but it will take us a century at the rate we're going.

Late in the afternoon the high cloudiness disappears and we move out from under the weather system that has had us trapped for so long. "Absolutely beautiful weather," says Steve on the evening radio schedule. "This first sunny afternoon gives the crew a chance to get things dry. Clothing is tied everywhere on the canoe for drying."

And it has been a beautiful day. Above the setting sun is a thin crescent moon with Venus close by. We've been traveling for four days and we're still only a hundred miles from where we started. We've been in sighting distance of Mauna Kea all this time but we haven't seen it. How easy it might have been for ancient navigators to have missed the islands in weather like this!

Ishka's instruments tell us that we're well past 18° N, moving southward at 3 to 4 knots as our 5th day dawns. Winds are 20 to 25 knots from the east and the sky is still overcast. It's good to be proceeding steadily along the way, not having to work so hard just to stay in place.

Hōkūle‘a shifts a thousand pounds forward to keep the bow low so that the canoe can point more directly into the wind.

"We're holding an ideal course thanks to the redistribution of weight," says Steve. "Usually steering is done by filling the sails with wind, trimming, and letting the canoe steer itself. Another way is using steering sweeps, lowering or raising a sweep to create a temporary keel. A third way is by shifting the weight as we're doing today."

At sunset we encounter what Mau considers "strong winds." Both Laehu and Lahope sails are lowered. In the process the forward boom cracks at its point of greatest curvature. Sea anchors are deployed to slow the drift, but even then the canoe drifts westward at a speed of one knot.

Tava and Leon help Mau put a splice on the boom and lash it with dacron line. The material is modern but the art is old. After three hours of down time the sail is hoisted and once again *Hōkūle'a* moves toward Tahiti.

No stars tonight. So far in these first five nights we've had only occasional glimpses of what lies beyond the clouds. How ironic for Nainoa to have based his wayfinding system on the stars and now they haven't yet appeared! Still he has a sense of where we are. Later when the stars do come out they simply give him greater certainty. He sums up the week's frustration:

Nainoa: Too many clouds, no stars. The wind is too strong from the east. We're always putting the sails up and down. It's raining all the time. I'm cold and I want to go home.
Steve: Other than that, Nainoa?
Nainoa: Oh, this is great. Lots of fun. I'm enjoying it.

And with that we move into a week of swift sailing.

Halcyon Days

*T*he storm is over. At dawn on the 6th day we're 200 miles south of Hilo and moving into warmer waters. Israel Kamoku's prophecy has been fulfilled—rough seas for the first 200 miles.

"We're starting the navigation as of sunrise today," says Nainoa, "using these parameters: three sailing days out of Hilo and three houses west of the line." He has mentally crossed out all the wandering and confusion of the last five days and has picked a point once more from which to begin.

Today the sun crosses the equator on its way into the Northern Hemisphere. It's the first day of spring, the time of vernal equinox. Traditionally it's a time of celebration, of feasts and festivals and rites of spring. An appropriate time to be starting anew.

"Weak but readable" is Honolulu Coast Guard's assessment of the strength of our signal. But that's no surprise since we're now 400 miles from Honolulu. We shift frequency from 4 to 8 megahertz, and on this shorter wavelength we come in "loud and clear."

"We're traveling a little faster than 5 knots," says Nainoa. "The wind has swung around to come in from the northeast. We sheeted-out the back sail; that gives us good speed. We can hold SW Manu easily. If we wanted to go higher into the wind we'd sheet-in the back sail."

Nainoa sees three swells. "The biggest and most consistent is NE Manu. It's running over and disguising the Hikina swell. The SE Manu swell is also there. I think it will be bigger tomorrow."

Hōkūleʻa has several fishing lines rigged, and already they have made several catches. Today *Ishka* hauls up its first. Mike uses a hammer to bash the sleek yellow-and-blue creature—*ahi* maybe—on the head. Trembling continues, then ceases, and we call the canoe on VHF offering to share the catch. No need, for they have a whole

135

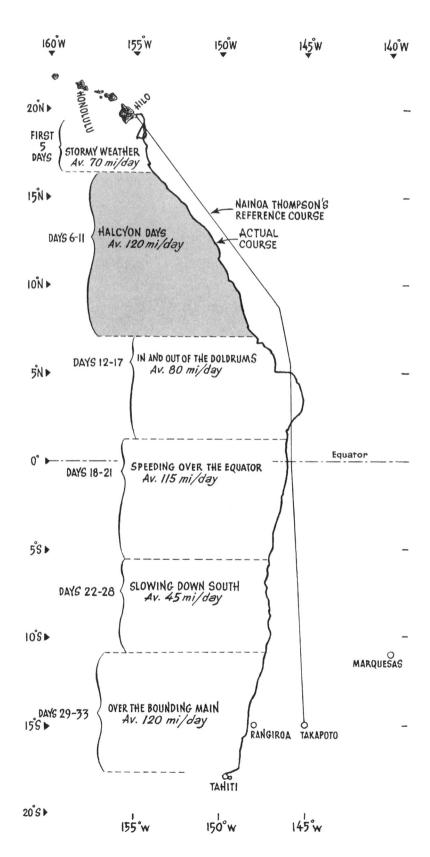

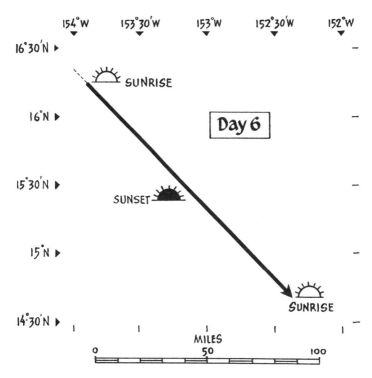

biological ecosystem traveling along with them beneath the canoe. By running long lines to deeper depth the nutritional needs for the entire voyage might possibly be met.

Nainoa tells us what he is learning of the winds from Mau: "When winds 'fight' there's a squall. The water gets 'jumpy' and the canoe slows down. But the squall may not be moving in the same direction as the dominant wind. The wind is always going to make you turn into it. When that squall came by last night, it tried to pull us into it, and we swung counterclockwise right around it."

The sun sets. We travel into the night at an average speed of 5.4 knots. Our course is SE Manu, slightly "up" from the direction of the reference course. We're gaining houses. "The islands are beginning to move on the compass. Tahiti is SE Haka, getting more Hema. The Cooks are between Haka and Na Leo, moving toward Na Leo. We're 14° north."

Our 7th day at sea begins with "Radio station KMI, this is Whiskey Hotel Alpha 9072, the *Ishka.*" One hundred watts of power heats the sloop's antenna causing it to radiate at wave lengths we

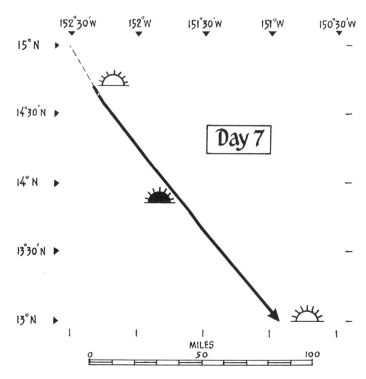

cannot see. A layer of ionized gas high above the earth's surface reflects that energy back to earth.

"*Ishka,* this is KMI. Give us a short count." While I count slowly "Five . . . four . . . three . . . two . . . one . . ." a huge directional antenna at Point Reyes in California, sweeping the sky for greatest signal intensity, homes-in on the radiating *Ishka.* "Stand by for a phone patch to Honolulu," says a pleasant voice.

The patch completed and we're instantly in thousands of cars and homes in Hawai'i telling of life aboard two vessels within a single circle of the sea. Each day radio station KCCN brings that intimate circle to the people of Hawai'i.

"Good morning, Skylark."

"Good morning, Will," responds the melodious voice of Jacqueline Leilani, the Honolulu Skylark, "How's it going out there at sea today?"

"Just fine. We're 340 miles southeast of Hilo and moving right along. Gordon thinks we're doing 8 knots. He calls it a 'real breakaway' after our slow week."

"And how's Nainoa doing?"

"He's right on, Skylark. There are difficulties. For instance, he's counted on using the stars but they've shown only briefly. And the weather; well, that's been bad except for today. Even the swells—he has been trying to keep direction by using them, but they've not been that good. He calls them 'bust-up' swells. Anyway, he sees us now as two houses west of his reference line and at a latitude of 13.5° N. That puts us within 80 miles of where instrument navigation says we are."

"That's amazing! So big an ocean and so few clues. Tell me, how's the fishing? People have been asking."

"Easy. *Hōkūle‘a* has plenty. Something big must be way down there because already they've lost several hooks. The lines just aren't strong enough."

"Tell me, Will, was that Venus I saw last night above the setting sun?"

"Beautiful, wasn't it? We watched it setting into the sea four hours after sunset. Jupiter, Mars, and Saturn were rising at about that time. Did you see them?"

"I'll look tonight. We have a message for you from the children of the Halau o Hale‘iwa. They're keeping track of where you are on their own Chart 526 of the Pacific. They're learning how big the ocean really is as they follow your progress. It gives them a greater understanding of their heritage. They send you all their fondest aloha."

"Thanks, Skylark. A message like that touches us all, way out here at sea. I'll relay it to *Hōkūle‘a*. Talk with you tomorrow. Aloha."

It is a good day, and we travel 130 miles southeast at a speed of 5.4 knots.

Our 8th day begins with, "Good morning, Skylark," and our circle expands 300-fold to include a million people in Hawai‘i.

"Good morning, Will. How are you doing out there today?"

"Just fine. We're now 500 miles from Hilo, 700 from Honolulu, and 800 from Kaua‘i."

"Wonderful!" comes back Skylark's voice. "Last night it was clear and I found Jupiter and Saturn in the east."

"We saw them, too, and thought of you there in Hawai‘i. Nainoa found a star that helps him in determining direction. It pairs

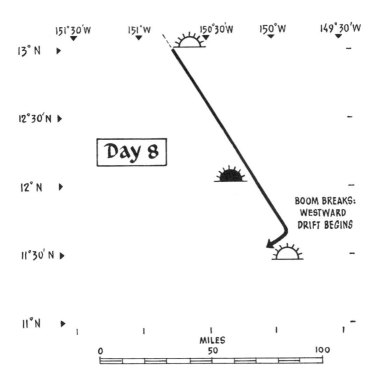

with Alpha Centauri as a meridional direction pointer. He doesn't have its official name so he's calling it the 'Willy Star.' "

"I'll bet he named it after you. How nice! Any more fish?"

"We caught an *ahi* yesterday, so we had sashimi and onions."

"How's Nainoa doing?"

"Right on. We've had good winds, and he thinks we're back on the reference course."

"And that runs right to Tahiti, I suppose."

"Actually to Takapoto in the Tuamotus. It's a line he has in mind, a way of staying oriented. Not a course to be sailed. Yesterday he gave us an estimated time of arrival in the Tuamotus of two weeks."

"Now that you're able to see the stars out there, how is Nainoa using them?"

"Last night he used two stars in the Little Dipper to determine latitude. He also used the Southern Cross."

Nathan Wong

"How beautiful to know where you are by the stars!"

"Just like the ancients. Talk with you tomorrow, Skylark. Aloha."

"A hui ho."

Radiation ceases and our thousand-mile electronic circle collapses into a 3-mile visual one. We relay pertinent information to *Hōkūleʻa*, and a morning report comes back:

Steve: What's our course this morning, Nainoa?

Nainoa: SE Manu. We just picked up by sheeting-in. I think we're doing 5 knots. Last night we were going fast, real fast.

Steve: Is there an ideal wind speed?

Nainoa: I find 25 knots comfortable, so that's ideal.

Steve: Something seems to be brewing on the horizon up ahead. What do you make of it?

Nainoa: Nothing serious. Low cumulus and high cirrus.

Steve: If Tahiti is Hema, then we're in the longitude of Tahiti—right?

Nainoa: Right. And I also think we're on the line. [Actually about 110 miles west of it.]

Steve: What are you using to steer by today?

Nainoa: I'm waiting for the moon. It's at First Quarter and will be rising at noon. When it gets too high I'll switch to the setting sun.

Steve: How do you determine wind speed?

Nainoa: From the surface of the water and the wind on my face. But that's an apparent wind due to the speed and direction of the canoe. . . . Oh, we're going south!

Steve: Has the wind shifted?

Nainoa: No, it's the steering. We're learning. It's a good crew—a real good crew and we're all learning.

Winds have been decreasing in strength all evening. At midnight, in relatively light wind, the boom breaks. Three days ago it cracked; now it is in two pieces.

Mau spends the next six hours in the light of flashlights, fashioning a scarf joint out of two pieces of boom. *Ishka* waits, sailing back and forth from horizon to horizon under the clearest sky we've seen so far. Crux is 8° higher than it was when we left Hawai'i. The Milky Way itself is a faint band of light arching from northeast to southwest across the heavens. A beautiful night.

The rising sail meets the rising sun at the beginning of our 9th day at sea. The boom is repaired and we're ready for another good day of sailing. But with the first wind on the sail, the boom breaks again and the sail is lowered.

Bracing pieces are put into place on the sides of the break and lashed. Again the sail is raised. This time there's a loud crack. Even though there's no visible break, down comes the sail.

"Honolulu COMSTA, *Hōkūle'a* is in a hove-to condition for minor repairs."

Mau tries a different method this time. Using an adz, he shapes a piece of wood to just the right curvature to match the scarfed ends of the original boom. His experienced eye is his guide—no measurement—and when completed the pieces fit together as perfectly as a glued joint.

While the repair work is going on Steve reports on damage that

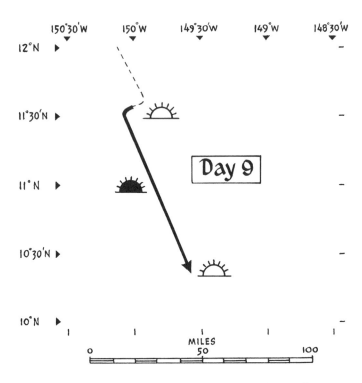

Hōkūleʻa has sustained on its first week at sea: "A steering sweep has broken, the Lahope sail has developed a small tear, and a crack has opened up along the bulkhead portions of the gunwale on the port side of each hull."

At noon the sail goes up and comes down. *Ishka* keeps sailing back and forth as it has been doing for the past twelve hours. (Later in the voyage the waiting will be reversed as *Hōkūleʻa* waits for its escort.) John Eddy steers, pushing *Ishka*'s tiller with his knees until he gets tired and hooks it onto the chain of the self-steering mechanism. Standing beneath the canvas canopy and holding onto the handrail above the galley, he checks the compass. Then he tugs on a line to adjust the windvane, muttering, "It, too, is becoming temperamental."

"*Hōkūleʻa* is now underway," says Steve on the VHF. We cheer the sight and a moment later the sail comes down. Quickly he reassures us, "No problem. It's only a matter of adjusting the rigging. Nainoa estimates a 12-mile westward drift during our half-day's

Marion Lyman and Jo-Anne Sterling

hove-to condition." Soon the wind once more fills the sails, and we're moving over the sea at 5 knots.

Nainoa tells Steve what he is learning about reading the sea. "Mau uses five swells—north, northeast, east, southeast, and south. Usually I see only three. If the wind is east then you get the east swell, but you also get one on either side—the northeast and southeast swells. If it's a northeast wind, you also get swells from the north and east."

Reading squalls is an art. Mau gives Nainoa the principles:

If the rain cloud is black, the wind is not strong. If the cloud is brown, the wind is probably strong. If the cloud is high, there's not much wind but maybe a lot of rain. If it's low, probably lots of wind. What you do is to sail up to it. The last clue is the color of the line at the surface of the water beneath the cloud. If it is black you know it is a real strong wind. If it's the same color as the ocean near you then it is not a strong wind. If the water is bumpy inside then you know there's a strong wind.

Nainoa has learned that Mau can see a change in the wind by the "road" of the clouds: "Clouds rise out of the horizon. Mau can tell a wind change long before it happens. I have yet to see that road."

Nainoa continually strives to know how Mau's system of navigation works. He understands the principles, and expresses his amazement metaphorically: "Mau knows direction like he knows the back of his hand. He knows waves like he knows an old friend. The waves show him the way no matter how they're covered up. Mau just looks at the ocean and he sees direction. He can't explain how he does it. He's an artist, a master. I can appreciate his art without being able to do it myself."

Nainoa calculates: "Atria is a little higher than Polaris so we must be about 10° N. Also Atria is as high above the horizon as it is from its pair star, 'Alex.' " Nainoa has honored *Ishka*'s captain in naming this previously unnamed star. "That's why I say we're about 10° N. The height of the Southern Cross shows us to be about 10° N. Also the 12° star with Polaris."

Steve reports at the beginning of our 10th day at sea, "We're sailing swiftly, surely, on the shining path of Kanaloa to Tahiti."

We make good progress during the day. In the evening twilight hour Nainoa expresses some thoughts:

We're surfing. The wind is constant, but the canoe is accelerating down the waves. We're dry. Nobody got wet today, right? White water breaks where the southeast and east swells meet. That's what had been breaking over the hull early this morning. Now that we're turned away from it, it doesn't reach the hull. We're in really choppy water with white water rolling backward in place, so I think we're at the edge of the countercurrent."

Steve: When do you expect to see the doldrums?
Nainoa: Anywhere within the next three days.
Steve: What is your plan when we reach the doldrums?
Nainoa: Go right on through fast as we can. Winds there come from any direction, but they're weak and don't last long.
Steve: Heavy cloud cover in the doldrums makes it difficult to keep direction.
Nainoa: Right. But I think I can tell direction by the waves. Besides, we're lucky to have a Full Moon to light the sea.

Nainoa spends day and night thinking about where *Hōkūleʻa* might be relative to his reference course. He analyzes:

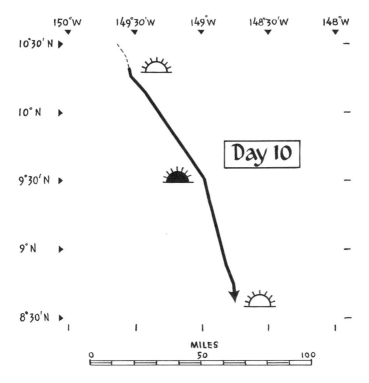

Our SE Na Leo course has set us another house down today. We went a half sailing day southeast Na Leo, and that's two houses down from Manu. Right now we're three houses west of the line. I don't like that. But if the countercurrent in the doldrums is one knot, then that's 24 miles a day to the east. If we stay in the doldrums for four days it will put us way up. We'll stay Na Leo for at least three more days instead of going Haka, and that will give us three days of easting. If we then go Na Leo for three days we'll be back on the line.

Nainoa uses logic and mathematics. And Mau? Does he rely upon a spatial intelligence for knowing the way and a bodily kinesthetic awareness for finding it? At any rate, two different ways converge in solving this problem of reaching Tahiti.

Nainoa thinks latitude: "Crux is three times higher than it is in Hawai'i, giving us a latitude of 9° N. The distance of Menkent to Beta Centauri and on to the horizon shows us about 8° north. Miaplacidus to Avior shows us about 9° N. Miaplacidus is 20° from the

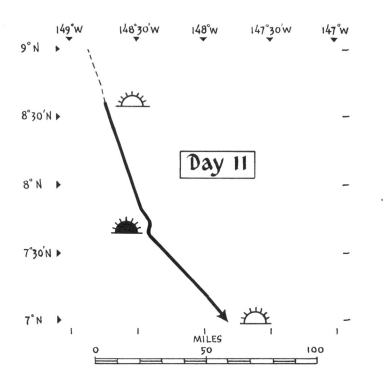

pole, and here where it is 11° above the horizon that means we're 9° N."

When Steve asks Nainoa on this mellow night if he has any other thoughts, Nainoa replies, "The wind seems to be guiding us down. Go to sleep and wait to see what happens. We might even land in Pape'ete."

Our 11th day at sea begins with a message from Marlene Among, executive secretary of the Polynesian Voyaging Society. Through KMI radio she tells us, "Kainalu Bertelmann was born March 24 at 11:51 A.M. Six pounds, 5 ounces, 19½ inches long. Both mother and son are fine and healthy."

We call *Hōkūle'a* on VHF. Lee relays the message to our newest father, Shorty Bertelmann, but he does not reply. He cannot. The impact is overwhelming, so far at sea, so far from home.

A light rain falls most of the day. *Hōkūle'a* captures 30 gallons of rain water in the catchment tarp. The water is put in reserve, for even though it is fresh and drinkable it has a taste of tarp.

"Looks as if we might not experience typical doldrum weather at this time," says Nainoa. "If we do not meet it in two days I think we'll not experience it at all."

Today the sea is white and choppy and the weather is warmer. Nainoa's interior monologue continues:

I think the wind is changing from NE Lā to SE Lā. Or it might be this white water is due to the countercurrent running against the wind. Anyway the canoe doesn't rock as it did before.

This has got to be the region of convergence where the trade winds meet. The ocean's surface is bent and deformed by the speed and direction of the wind. Here it's not like the regular open ocean. Up to now the motion of the canoe has been sharp and abrupt with lots of splashing. Now that has gone but our direction hasn't changed that much.

I really don't think that this is the doldrums. If it were, we'd have a calm sea with good open ocean swells. Maybe the countercurrent has something to do with this condition. Surely we didn't go from one current to another in a day.

Mau and I talked about the doldrums and the spinning clouds. Warm air rises, spinning counterclockwise in the doldrums due to the earth's rotation. You can actually see that spinning. For the navigator it's significant. You can know where you are relative to the winds if you can tell what direction the lows are from you.

Jo-Anne Sterling tells Steve about her feelings for *Hōkūleʻa:*

I have lots of respect for this canoe. I talk to her, take care of her. She loves to go. It's amazing to watch her. Sometimes she goes goofy, then gets out of it. She comes alive at sea. It seems as if we're being drawn to Tahiti. Nobody is steering. Sails are set and we're going. She's taking us there.

Down in the compartment I listen to the sounds at night. Familiar sounds. When the winds are high and the sea is rough she feels as if she's 120 feet long instead of 60. She can make herself look so small and pathetic on the big ocean. But then she can also make herself look big and fly like a bird.

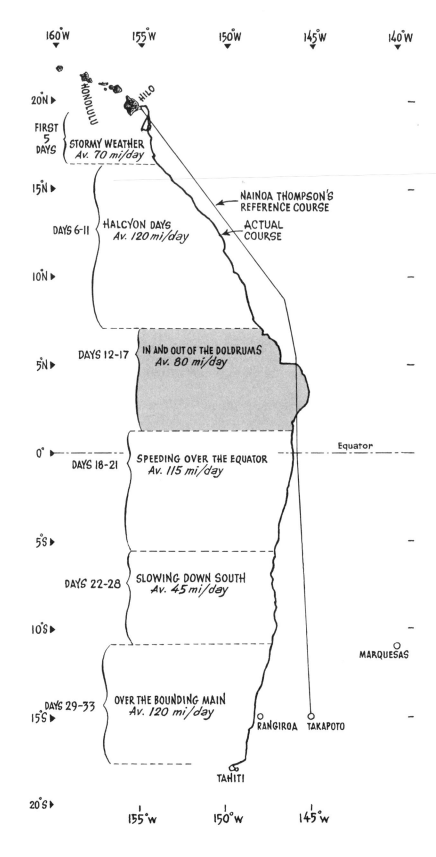

In and out of the Doldrums

Steve reports to us at sunrise on the 12th day: "Last night we found that we were actually going east when we thought we were going south. Clouds were heavy. For a few moments the cut of the moon and the position of Jupiter gave us direction. Not much else.

"This morning at 0120," Steve continues (and we chuckle at his reference to time, since all timepieces were stowed away in a sealed container), "we caught a pair of wet blue jeans belonging to Mr. Harry Ho. The highly unusual catch is to be attributed to the effectiveness of the fishhook carved from bone by crew member Mr. Sam Ka'ai."

Winds are weakening. The weather station tells us that gale force winds are still whipping Hawai'i, and a tropical cyclone is active in the Southern Hemisphere at the latitude of Tahiti. No threat is it to us, since it's too far west to bother. We'll watch, though, for a swell from that storm that might reach us in a few days. If *Hōkūle'a*'s crew sees it, they may infer the presence of a disturbance that we aboard *Ishka* know about right now.

Skylark appears at 0715 along with the KCCN community. We send a happy birthday greeting to Pat Aiu's daughter, Puaala, who is seventeen years old today. Gordon has a message of thanks to Lt. Beverly Kelley of *Cape Newagen* for Coast Guard assistance that night off the Hāmākua coast. We send our aloha to the people of Hawai'i, little realizing that this is our last radio transmission through KMI.

Progress is slow. "Hundred percent cloud cover," says Nainoa. "It's overcast and we have a little rain, heavy at times. We're not navigating but drifting . . . sideways . . . backwards . . . going all over the place. I think that we're going east, south, southeast, southwest, but I don't know exactly when."

We're in the doldrums. Nainoa has had persistent dreams about

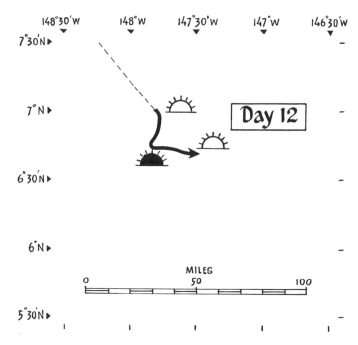

being stuck here and becoming disoriented. The sun beats down intensely upon this Intertropical Convergence Zone and heats the ocean. The air is warm and moist. The doldrums is a belt of calm between the northeast and southeast trade wind systems that can trap a sailing vessel for days or weeks at a time. It's also a region notorious for spawning severe forms of weather—squalls, thunderstorms, and huge violent cyclonic disturbances.

"I know the wind has changed," says Nainoa, "but I don't know what it has changed to. All I can do is to feel the swell. Both sails are up and we have variable speed and direction. The crew is lackadaisical, reflecting the spirit of this weather. Dear Will, I quit. I'm going home. Steve is now our navigator. Goodbye."

Two in the afternoon. We're in the lulling, bobbing, rocking, dreamy doldrums. Alex stops *Ishka*'s engines, and for the first time in two weeks we hear the strange sound of silence. Not for long, for soon the stereo system produces the voices of Robert and Roland Cazimero blending in exquisite harmony—sounds on this languid sea evoking images of the lambent hula of Leinaala Heine Kalama.

Then Roland sings these words from "Doldrum Blues," written

by Keli'i Tau'a, that he has set to music in the album *"Hōkūle'a,"* honoring the previous voyage:

> I've traveled halfway to Tahiti.
> As I sit and ponder, this is a turning point for me.
> Recall the past or look to the future?
> My Doldrum Blues sing cheerfully;
> The winds bring forth the answer.

The tape runs out, a breeze comes up, and we await the answer. Alex starts the engines. Buzz. He touches the starter button again. Buzz. He removes the deck plates and goes below to see what the problem is. Nothing obvious. Once more he touches the starter button. Buzz. Blue smoke billows through the chart room and three carbon dioxide fire extinguishers converge from three different directions. Fortunately we don't have to use them, but we are given to a moment's reflection upon the vulnerability of a vessel on fire at sea and, in this case, the irony of it all if the escort crew should have to continue to Tahiti aboard its charge.

Alex inspects the engine and finds a warm, burned-out starter. He then does a thorough step-by-step examination of the engine, checking and cleaning electrical contacts with emery cloth. During shutdown, and due to an unusual distribution of weight on the boat, water may have entered the engine. Leon lends his diesel expertise, but repairs cannot be completed at sea and *Ishka* becomes solely dependent on sail power for the rest of the journey.

We drift west and south today. At sunset a wind springs up from the west, not a strong one but a pleasing wind that carries us directly east. And during this night of the great west wind we watch a waxing gibbous moon move past Mars to join Regulus.

Sunrise on our 13th day at sea and we're 25 miles straight east of where we were last night at sunset. *Ishka*'s engines are silent and we do not use the radio transmitter. A few days before we left Hawai'i, Roy Yee, head of the communications committee, had told us, "You miss one schedule, and that's not bad. Two times, and we're worried. Three times, and we start looking for you." I inform the

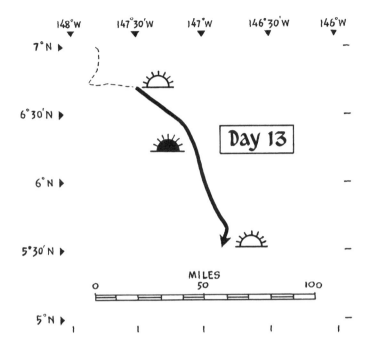

captains of our two missed schedules and send a message to Honolulu COMSTA:

> Starter motor under repair. Cannot recharge batteries at this time.
> Conserving battery power. Both vessels otherwise normal. Proceeding
> on course. Listening at 0715 and 1615 for messages. Transmitting only
> in emergency until recharging capability is restored.

We maintain VHF contact with *Hōkūle'a* on regular morning and
evening schedules or upon the flashing of the signal mirror. VHF is
low power transmission, and in the interest of conserving battery
power we keep communication curt.

"The NNE swell is the big one today but decreasing in intensity,"
reports Nainoa. "We also have the NE Manu and Hikina swells.
With the wind shifting to the east we're getting a bigger SE Manu
swell."

Ishka raises a genoa job sail, or "jenny," to catch more wind and
keep pace with *Hōkūle'a*. The two vessels are striking in contrast and
concept. *Hōkūle'a*'s loaded weight is 11 tons; *Ishka*'s is 28. *Ishka* is

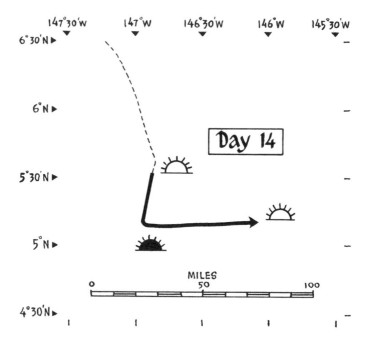

carrying an extra burden of weight in provisions and water for both vessels. The double-hulled canoe is a stable platform riding on the surface of the sea; the mono-hull plows through the waves. Stability is maintained in one by two separate hulls and crab-claw sails; in the other by a deep hull with a heavily weighted keel. Alex has deliberately reduced the sail area of *Ishka* so that sailing the 48-foot sloop can be a one-person operation. While *Ishka*'s engines were working, keeping up with *Hōkūleʻa* was no problem. Now it is.

Late in the afternoon winds increase in strength, and Nainoa's spirit soars: "I think we're in the SE trades and out of the doldrums. We're moving okay in this light wind, about 3.5 knots. I like the doldrums. Going back is going to be a treat."

Shortly after sunrise on our 14th day at sea, Honolulu Coast Guard relays a message from Roy Yee:

Suggest you remove and transfer battery from *Hōkūleʻa*. Canoe has three 12-volt batteries that could be used by *Ishka*. They have batteries for hand-held radio. I calculate 16 days battery life assuming 30 percent leakage. Battery life could be extended. We would appreciate condition report every other day at your discretion. Receiving satellite position on your course.

They're watching us; they know where we are. Dixon Stroup and the Scripps Oceanographic Institute have seen to it that the ARGOS satellite navigating system is measuring *Hōkūleʻa*'s position several times a day. Aboard the canoe is a transponder—a radio transmitter sealed in a long plastic tube—sending signals up to orbiting satellites. When a satellite travels over France it dumps the data into a computer in France that Bernie Kilonsky accesses on a computer at the Mānoa Campus of the University of Hawaiʻi. The read-out gives the date and time of fix, the canoe's latitude, longitude, speed, course, and distance traveled since the last fix.

Winds are weak, swells are prominent, and we spend the day moving slowly southward at 2 knots. Nainoa reports: "Swells are real evident today—NE Manu, SE Manu, and Hikina. My strategy is to steer way to the east. I want to make up for current drift caused by our staying out here extra days. We still have to go east more than we go west."

The sun sets, Venus reflects upon the sea, and a gibbous moon passes within a degree of Jupiter. Another southwest wind springs up, and during the night we travel eastward at a speed of 4.5 knots.

Nainoa adjusts to this unusual condition: "We're going Hikina—straight east. So that's Lā, ʻĀina, Noio, Manu, Nalani, Na Leo, Haka—seven houses of deviation from the reference course. Seven, and then there's the current. So when you think seven, you've got to think five." Steve is silent, stunned by a message that is as internally consistent in Nainoa's mind as it is externally absurd.

A strange, low-level cloud surrounds us at midnight, coming in quietly like a fog from the north. Skies are overcast, lightning flashes, and the moon wears a halo.

Sunrise on our 15th day at sea finds us running ahead of small clouds—dark, ominous clouds, and we search them for waterspouts. Their bases are ragged, not smooth, and if we understand Mau, that's a sign of little wind.

We've lost our west wind. The only wind this morning is, says Nainoa,

one coming out of that squall line, an erratic wind that is varying widely. The change in wind and weather is so quick that you know that this cannot be a regular system. I think that the dominant wind is NE Manu because of the big wave coming from that direction. The water is choppy, real choppy, and I think that it is the effect of the doldrums. But I think we're getting out of it because the wind is switching more to the east and the water is mellowing out.

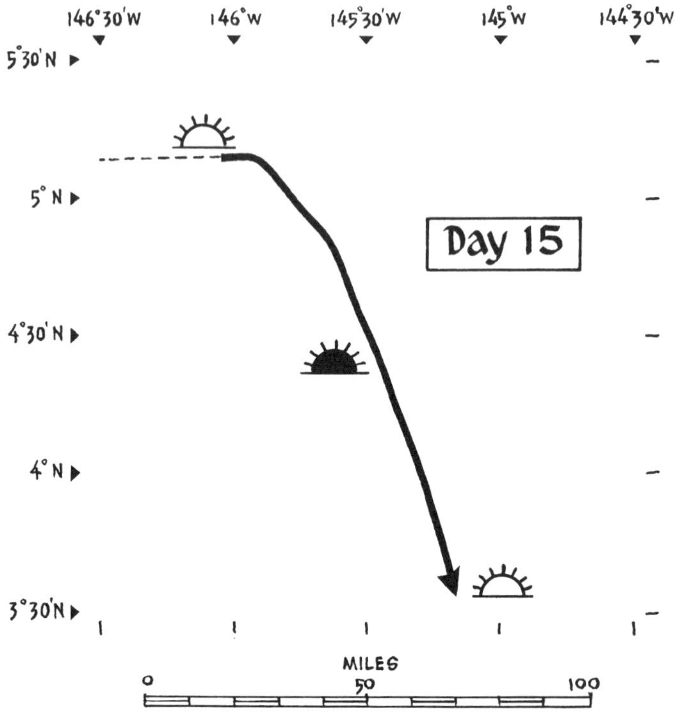

We move into a squall. Beneath this cloud umbrella is darkness so great that we cannot see to work in *Ishka*'s chart room. No sun; even though it is directly overhead at noon, there's no trace of it. During the past week we've had only one starry night, yet Nainoa seems to know where he is. At times his estimate of latitude may be off by a degree, but that's of no consequence here in a big ocean so far from land.

Nainoa continues:

I look at Mau's navigational statements. Lots of what he says doesn't make mathematical sense to me. But it works for him and has enabled his survival. Mathematics misses when we try to understand what he does.

His system works for him without a doubt. The five waves he sees are always there for him, though I might not find them. The reference birds, too, they're also always there to guide him to the land.

My system makes sense to me. Whether it works or not we'll soon know. So far it's working and I'm learning. That's why we're out here—to learn. I got through the doldrums without help, and I feel good about that. One cloudy night, though, it was so black that I couldn't see any swell at all. Later the Full Moon lighted the northeast swell, so then I knew directions.

We're now four houses east of the line. Tonight we'll run Na Leo and by morning will be five houses east. Then we'll stay east, and when we get to the equator, I'll make up my mind what to do from there on.

Steve: At what point are you going to alert the crew to keep a sharp lookout for land?

Nainoa: From 7° to 10° south we'll look for the Marquesas. From 10° to 12° we'll look for Caroline, Vostok, and Flint islands. And from 13° on, we'll look for the Tuamotus and Societies.

Steve: Given that we're four houses east of the line, there's not much chance, is there, of seeing those islands?

Nainoa: No. But we'll look anyway because it's not going to hurt to look. I really might be wrong.

Steve: What's your gut feeling about it—are you right or wrong?

Nainoa: I feel that we're four houses east of the line.

Our plotting of position from information gathered through instruments aboard *Ishka* shows that we reach our greatest distance east of the reference course at sunrise on our 16th day at sea. Nainoa has no way of knowing longitude, but he reports perceived directions to islands through Steve:

Direction to the Marquesas, SE Na Leo; Tahiti, SW Haka; the Cooks, SW Nalani; and Hawai'i, NW Na Leo. We're beneath the star Mira, 3° 30′ N latitude. *Hōkūle'a* status, excellent. Course, SE Haka. Speed, 2 knots. Wind speed, 5–10 knots from Hikina. Principal swells, NE Manu, Hikina, 'Ākau, and SE Manu. Clouds are high cirrus. No trade wind clouds. Cloud cover, 30 percent. ETA first landfall, twelve days. We're moving steadily, not terribly fast. We're off the wind, so each crew member is taking a turn at the windward steering paddle.

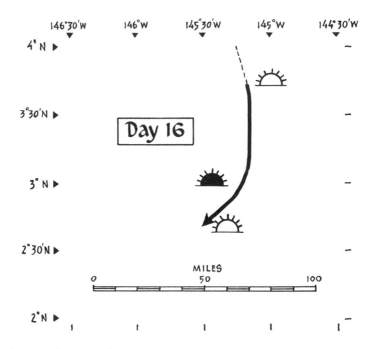

Chad Baybayan talks with Steve, telling of his interest in *Hōkūleʻa:*

I was going to school up in Oregon when I read an article that had Herb
Kane's paintings of Polynesian canoes in it. I got all excited about the idea,
and the day I got back home to Maui, *Hōkūleʻa* also arrived. I was only
eighteen then. Next year I helped Sam Kaʻai with the ʻawa ceremony for
the 1976 Tahiti departure.

After the 1978 mishap, I worked on *Hōkūleʻa* as part of the Alu Like
program. We raised the gunwales on the canoe, worked on the mast, gaff,
and boom. We also did a lot of caulking. We had no pattern for the boom,
so we drew one on the floor of the canoe house up at Kamehameha
Schools. Then we went into the woods to cut *hau* wood. But that didn't
work, so we bought wood and laminated it for the boom.

This trip is the high point in my life so far. I've learned so much in so
short a time. I like the companionship of people and the good feeling of
being out here on the ocean with them. We've experienced lots of things
that have made us better sailors, like the breaking and the repairing of the
boom. I'm enjoying each moment fully, and I'm not looking forward to
the end of the trip. It will happen, of course, and then this feeling will be
in the past. I'm happy right now—and we haven't passed the equator yet.

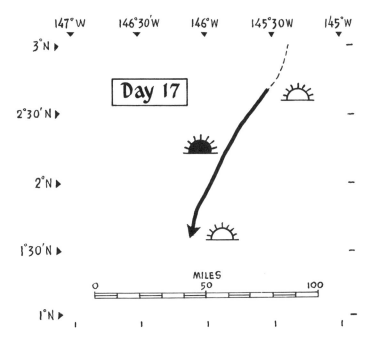

Squalls around us begin dissipating and we enjoy a cloudless afternoon. We're moving steadily southward, "not terribly fast." It's a lazy day with not much happening when suddenly out of nowhere Elsa brings out of the galley a Sunday afternoon treat of brown bread. We stand the 1615 radio watch and hear Kodiac COMSTA calling the cutter *Polar Sea*. San Francisco COMSTA is calling *Cape Corwin*. And Honolulu COMSTA? Nothing.

Hōkūleʻa trices her sails at sunset; *Ishka* takes hers down. It's a calm night. Very light breeze, perhaps 2 knots. A Full Moon is rising on a flat sea. We're again drifting, bobbing, nodding. *Hōkūleʻa* is first on our port, then starboard, then at our bow and stern as we circle around each other. Round and round we go, phantom-like, waiting. John and Mike break out mandolin and guitar, and on *Ishka*'s forecastle in the light of a Full Moon improvise a song, "I've got the doldrum blues on a NE Manu swell," and we enjoy a pacific night while waiting for the wind.

Big flat swells are rolling under us like an infinite succession of undulating Mauna Loas on this morning of our 17th day at sea. *Ishka*'s instruments tell us we're drifting westward 30 miles a day

Tava Taupu and Kainoa Lee at the steering sweep

while also moving south at twice that speed. Only the sound of small waves lapping against the hull and dish water splashing into the ocean break the spell of this sleep-generating scene.

Alex turns *Ishka*'s engines by hand; they respond slightly. Every day he turns them just a little, hoping for a gradual readjustment that will shake them out of their dormancy.

So quiet. Water trickles and bubbles against *Ishka*'s hulls. Alex asks first mate Mike to play music on the stereo system. A pilot light glows as a wonderful electro-mechanical system aboard a steel sloop begins pumping the happy and vibrant sounds of the Brandenburg concertos into the torpid air above an undulating, sand-duned sea . . . taking us back two and a half centuries and a half-world away to Bach in Brandenburg . . . and, even six centuries before that, back to the days of Albert the Bear, who conquered the tiny village of Brandenburg at a time when great Gothic cathedrals were being built in Europe, and Polynesian voyagers were right here where *Hōkūle'a* is now, the canoe "as idle as a painted vessel on a painted sea," and watched over by orbiting satellites that unhide the canoe and tell the world our latitude and longitude and speed.

Aboard *Hōkūleʻa*, Nainoa's mind is anything but inert. He explains to Steve: "I want to look for the North Star tonight. We might see it, but I doubt it. When Alkaid is high, as it will be tonight, Polaris is three-quarters of a degree below the north celestial pole. We're now so close to the equator that we'll see the North Star only just before sunrise or just after sunset, if we see it at all."

Nainoa's reference course allows for 22.5 days from Hilo to first landfall in the Tuamotus. Subtracting the number of days he expects *Hōkūleʻa* to spend in the equatorial countercurrent leaves 19 days exposed to a west-setting current that he figures will move the canoe westward 16 miles a day.

Tava Taupu talks with Steve. Tava was born and raised in Nuku Hiva in the Marquesas. He lived for three years in Tahiti. For the past nine years he has lived in Hawaiʻi. "I have five brothers, one dead; and six sisters, one dead. I'm the third youngest in the family."

Steve: And you have a birthday this coming week?
Tava: Yes. I think it will be in the water between Tahiti and the Tuamotus—6th day of April at home in the Marquesas.
Steve: Good trip? Good crew?
Tava: Yes.
Steve: And your bunk—is it dry?
Tava: Yah. The bunk is dry. Seven days we stay in the water. Cramp my leg. Cold. Cramp my leg inside the hole.

The Full Moon is rising. Tava calls it *yeahotunui*. When it is crescent, he calls it *meʻama hou*. The New Moon is *hokeke*, "dark moon."

He speaks of his love of sailing, and comments on the wind:

If the wind stays like this, maybe midnight the wind come more down and in the morning come back again. The wind is slow. Not too strong. Steady. It doesn't come one time. No one time, *pau*. Maybe three to four hours stay like this.

I'm really happy because I see the whole sky at night. Like inside the bowl. You're the center. There's nothing—front, back, side. My first time in the open ocean and I learn about stars. I just think more better for me I rest in the ocean now before no more ocean.

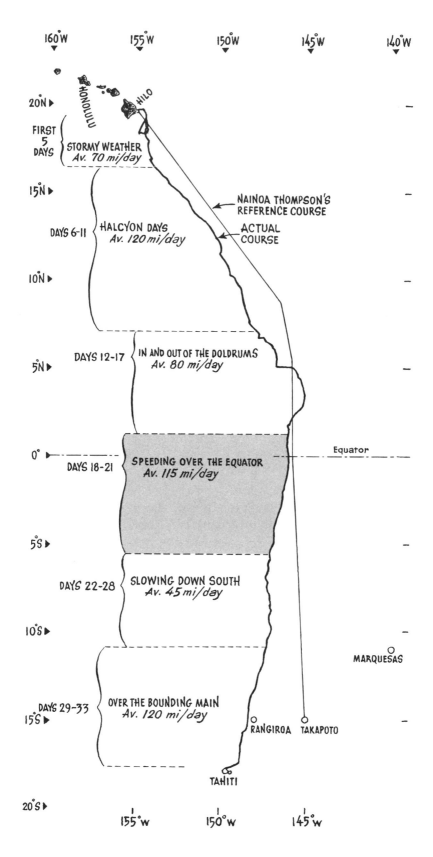

Speeding over the Equator

*W*e are within 2° of the equator as the sun rises on our 18th day at sea. Nainoa reports: "Last night I looked at Atria, Musca, Kochab, Miaplacidus, and the 18° star and 20° star in Draco. All showed us to be 2° N. We're getting the regular wave patterns back. A straight wind is coming from a little south of east. Lines of cumulus cloud are in the southeast, but they're tilted forward, not backward as trade wind clouds usually are. Everything is smooth—the water, the winds, the clouds."

Coast Guard Cutter *Polar Sea* is calling San Francisco. Honolulu is calling *Cape Newagen*. Nobody is calling us, so we terminate our 1615 listening schedule.

On the evening report from *Hōkūle'a,* Nainoa tells of interesting events and observations:

I went to sleep today. I'm getting overconfident. I don't have the intensity. If I lose it, I lose it. It's just an emotion. I have no control over it. Today it was hot and I was just lullabying all day long. We were going along in a straight line and everything was fine. Then I went to sleep for two hours. That kind of blew me away because when I woke up the wind had changed—drastically. I was mad for having slept so long. I'm not going to do that again. No more than one hour of sleep at a time for me. I'm going to sleep on the deck, not on the cushions, so that when my head falls onto the wooden deck I'll wake up.

He describes the characteristics of *Hōkūle'a* in a calm sea:

When the canoe doesn't leave the water, when it sits in the water in a trough and rides in and out, then that's when you get a lot of speed. When there's lots of wind and you're bucking a head wave, you lose speed. The canoe stops when it hits the wave. The sail luffs, and it takes time for it to

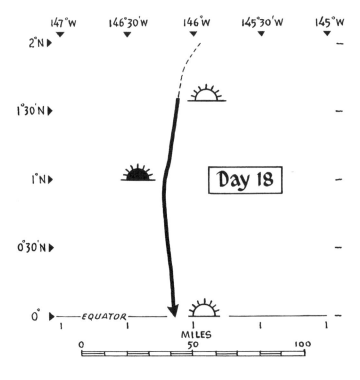

fill again and get back up to full speed. But when you have a calm sea, you really make ground. The canoe sits in the water; the sails stay full and do not luff.

Well before midnight he reports: "We're now heading for the rising Southern Cross, SE Na Leo. The wind changed with the last squall and we dropped to 4 knots. When the wind passes we'll hit straight wind, maybe 5.5 knots. I think that we'll cross the equator at sunrise tomorrow."

At sunrise on our 19th day at sea we do indeed cross the equator.

Steve reports: "We're moving along at 5 knots. Status of *Hōkūle'a,* excellent, superb—normal!" Nainoa adds, "Perfect! There's only one principal swell this morning, NE Manu. It's small and fragmented and comes only once in a while. If the wind holds we'll make a Tuamotu landfall in seven and a half days."

Mau and Nainoa have separated, not isolated, themselves from each other, as it must be on a voyage of learning. Mau is Nainoa's

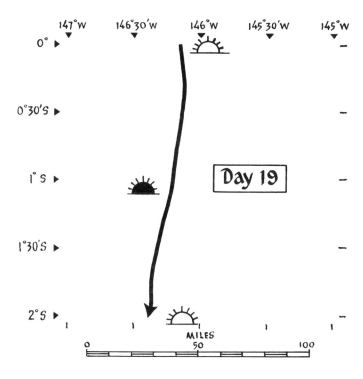

teacher, helping him learn the ways of the sea and always present in the event of difficulty. He does not take part in the navigation. Nainoa must learn for himself. It must not be easy for Mau to stand by and watch Nainoa make decisions that he would not have made, and to see him not see that which is obvious to him. But this is the way it must be: Nainoa is learning.

At first, Nainoa found this distancing between them artificial and uncomfortable. "But when I really took charge and decided to get on with the navigation I found Mau sleeping longer hours."

Being at the equator this time of year is an advantage in maintaining direction: "Good thing that the sun's nearly due east because I can use it for direction until almost noon—about eleven—and pick it up again after one in the afternoon."

Nainoa distinguishes between seas and swells: "Swells are big waves generated by pressure systems far beyond the horizon, and they maintain direction for long periods of time. But seas are generated by local winds. Seas generally come downwind, but they may be off by as much as 30° on either side of the wind. When the wind changes they get a bit more mish-mash."

Pat Aiu, the medical doctor aboard *Hōkūleʻa,* is the eleventh in a family of eleven. He tells Steve of his family's interest in sailing. A century ago when Hawaiʻi was a kingdom, the Aiu's owned double-hulled canoes and sailed them from Kailua-Kona to Lahaina, and even on to Oʻahu. His recent interest in *Hōkūleʻa* came through carpenter John Kruse who made the 1976 trip.

I've never sailed on a long voyage before, so I didn't know what to expect on this rather open vessel. I had no way of garnering the kind of medical information I'd need prior to coming aboard. The supplies I brought had to cover a broad area but in a limited amount because of space considerations. My experience, along with that of Dr. Wong's [he'll be aboard on the return trip], will give us a good knowledge of the needs on future voyages.

For instance, I certainly did not have in mind the amount of staphylo-coccal skin infection we would be seeing on this trip. I think that at least 80 percent of the crew has come down with it already. Fortunately, the crew itself is a very healthy bunch of people. All are personally very neat hygienically, so we've been able to overcome the problem. A potentially serious health problem that could have cropped up was food poisoning, but nothing came up. Everyone is healthy, but we've had a number of fungal problems and the usual motion sickness.

I really enjoy the sunny days. We've been in constant rain for a while and that gets me down. I see from this trip why men in the past were lured to the sea. It is a pleasant mode of travel if you're not concerned with time or speed—and if you can get some sunny days.

Pat sees himself first as a crew member, then as a person with experience and talent in dealing with injuries and seeing to the general health of the crew.

We're flying along on our 20th day at sea as the sun comes up in a sky nearly devoid of clouds. Far in the distance are a few patches of trade wind clouds hugging the horizon. That's all. Winds are brisk, about 18 knots. The sea is warm and there's a beauty in the monot-onous regularity of sea and sky with "warm tropic breezes kissing your skin," as Alex expresses it in his poetic way.

Two very different types of navigation are taking place on these two vessels. One uses instruments for gathering data; the other, only

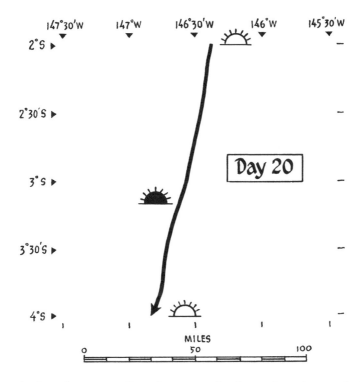

the mind and senses. One is external; the other, internal. One spreads a net over the earth and locates position relative to the intersection of imaginary lines that we call latitude and longitude. The other sees the navigator as at the center of sea and sky, with islands moving along that circle's edge.

Finding our position using instruments is a matter of comparing our local sky with that of England at the same moment. The difference in where the stars are in those two skies is a measure of where in the world we are—how far north or south of the equator, how far east or west of Greenwich. Because it is external, instrument navigation requires the use of an accurate timepiece, a means of measuring the angular height of a star above the horizon (a sextant), and a set of astronomical tables from which we determine where a star may be at any particular moment.

The wayfinder, on the other hand, knows where he starts and where he wants to go. Along the way he maintains continuous orientation by reading nature's signs and attending to the speed and

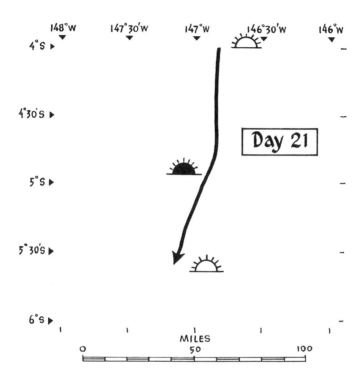

direction. If a storm comes up and the wayfinder loses direction, he's lost. Really lost. After the storm he re-orients as best he can and proceeds on the way. The instrument navigator, on the other hand, finds position after the storm by measuring where the stars are, provided the timepiece is still working and the sextant is still aboard.

Each time Steve interviews Nainoa he radios the information to us for back up. Nainoa tells the direction in which he perceives Hawai'i to be, also the Marquesas, Tuamotus, Societies, and the Cooks. He gives latitude to a high degree of precision from the elevation of stars. He reports where he thinks the canoe to be relative to his reference course. The sum of the data gives us a region, sometimes a large one and sometimes small—a region of the ocean, not a point, where he knows the canoe to be. We take all these bits of data and, picking a most probable point, connect points of probability into a line we call the canoe's presumed course.

We're moving straight south at 5.4 knots as the rising sun touches the sails of *Hōkūle'a* on this, the beginning of our 21st day at sea.

Harry Ho

Mau forecasts a mild shower two hours before it happens. He, Buddy, and Tava are making coconut drinking bowls. They caught another fish today and are sending it to us in a bucket.

All day long the two vessels travel close together. Some days are like that; companionship then seems okay. But at other times and for reasons we are not aware of, we prefer distance. We move apart, so far apart that the canoe's sails are then only tiny inverted triangles on the horizon. And at times we see only the tops of its sails.

How does proximity influence navigation? Nainoa would prefer a clean horizon, navigating in complete isolation. But that cannot be on this voyage with ''constant visual contact'' a criterion of escort. Nainoa feels that he is not affected by the presence of the escort. He also believes that Mau is little affected by it, simply doing what he does and crossing the escort out of his mind.

Steve: How does Mau determine latitude?

Nainoa: From the Big Dipper, Little Dipper, and the Southern Cross.

Steve: And the zenith star?

Nainoa: He doesn't care about zenith stars. He considers that playing around. The concept of zenith star has no meaning for him.

Steve: The Marquesas are now in SE Manu, moving into Hikina. Right?

Nainoa: Right. They're moving fast because they're so close. The Tuamotus are straight south, and they'll not be moving at all except for current.

Early in the evening Nainoa determines latitude to be 5° south: ''I'm amazed how fast the stars in the north are sinking and those in the south are rising. It's strange watching the stars near the equator. The other night Alpha and Beta Centauri came up perpendicular to the horizon. That can happen only near the equator. Mirzam and Canopus synchronously set. That, too, can happen only near the equator.''

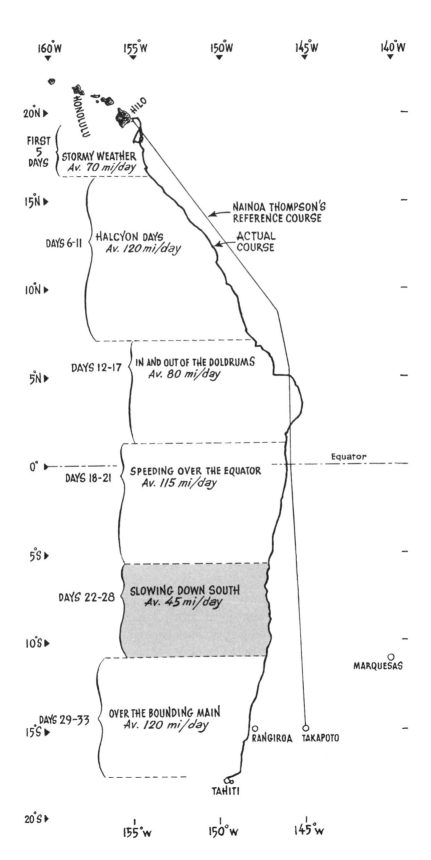

Slowing down South

*A*t dawn on our 22nd day at sea Steve describes life aboard the *Hōkūleʻa:*

As morning twilight begins, our navigator peers toward the eastern horizon, looking for clues to navigation and weather. The rising point of the sun is useful to him in determining the direction of *Hōkūleʻa* relative to the swells of the day. He also looks at clouds to predict the weather.

So with dawn our watch changes. Each team is on six hours and off six hours. The on-coming watch is awakened and they groggily adjust to the conditions of the canoe and the early morning weather. Breakfast is prepared in the galley that is located in the center of the deck between Laehu and Lahope sails. The menu is sometimes a sardine mixture on crackers. On another morning it might be scrambled eggs with bacon bits, bread, and cheese.

After breakfast the galley duties are attended to—washing stainless steel bowls, knives, forks, spoons, and cooking pots. All of this washing is done using sea water scooped out of the ocean in 2-gallon buckets tied to cords. Washing is done near the stern. The dishes are then put away and the galley secured. The off-crew has a chance to sleep or to attend to personal needs, such as brushing teeth or taking a bath in the forward net, or writing in journals. During the first ten days, duties included drying out clothes, the *lauhala* mats, and air mattresses.

The new crew coming on watch has duties to perform that are simple. They must be on deck, awake, and ready to help trim the sails by adjusting the sheets. [A sheet is a line, not a sail.] Depending on the wind, the sails may have to be triced and sometimes lowered completely onto the deck.

The sun climbs higher and things begin to dry. But an occasional wave breaks over the canoe and drenches the almost-dried articles.

Lunch is prepared. It might be a hot or cold lunch. Fourteen bowls are passed around to the crew, all of whom look forward to the second meal of the day. The food preparation persons are principally Buddy McGuire and Jo-Anne Sterling.

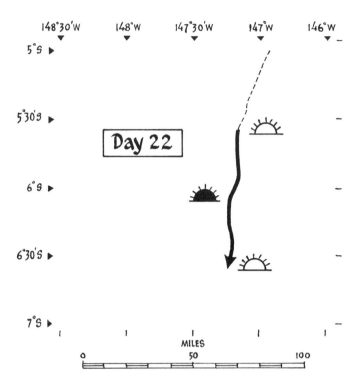

Afternoon, and a greater number of crew are out sunning, writing in log books, drawing, talking, and generally enjoying life at sea on an open-decked vessel.

Late afternoon and the sun is nearing the horizon. Then elaborate preparations are made for the largest meal of the day. After dinner Nainoa shares with the gathered crew his thoughts about the navigation and course. The meeting ends and the crew on watch remains on deck. The off-crew may linger and talk or play guitar before drifting off into their individual compartments to get rest before going on watch at midnight.

The on-crew checks the running lights and buttons up their foul-weather gear. Each night the wind picks up at about the time of evening meal, and it usually continues throughout the night. If stars are visible we check our course relative to them. We've not steered much but when we do, we trade off about every 20 minutes.

During the evening watch, crew members take time to enjoy a cup of coffee, tea, or hot chocolate along with crackers. The galley has a two-burner kerosene-burning Primus stove where we heat the water. Much of the time is spent in the galley or on the afterdeck, the crew feeling the motion of the canoe and observing the stars.

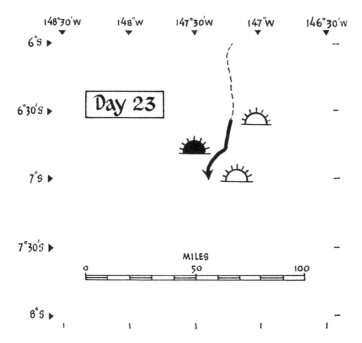

As midnight approaches, the watch crew prepares a fresh batch of hot water for the on-coming crew. The changing of the watch is perhaps most formal at midnight. The navigator informs the watch captain that it is midnight. Those going off watch awaken their relief persons, usually their bunk mate. After a period of transition in which both watch teams are out on deck adjusting to the motion of the vessel, the off-watch takes to their compartments usually rather quickly at this time of night.

The midnight-to-dawn watch hasn't much to do except trim the sails and pump the forward compartments when needed. The permanently mounted pumps are in the forward and aft compartments of each hull. During the strongest winds and roughest seas the frequency of pumping is about once every half-hour. When hove-to, no pumping is needed. Under normal sailing conditions pumping is done about every two hours.

The watch ends with the navigator peering toward the eastern horizon for clues to daytime direction and weather.

"Another day, another doldrum," sighs John Eddy at *Ishka*'s wheel on the morning of our 23rd day at sea. He pulls on a line to adjust the wind-vane mechanism that is completely inoperable in this light air.

John Eddy

We time a bubble as it moves alongside *Ishka* and calculate our speed to be 0.63 knots—a torpid tempo on a flat and glassy sea. Scattered around us are isolated puffs of cumulus clouds, but there are no lines of clouds anywhere to raise our hopes for a return of the winds. Slight swells rock our vessel as sails flip-flop from one side of the mast to the other.

The shortwave radio is turned on and WWVH in Maui beeps the seconds as Alex and Elsa prepare to take a noontime sight on the sun. A voice interrupts the beeping: "It is now 22 hours, 24 minutes Coordinated Universal Time." The beeping resumes and a low bass tone accompanies the 440-cycle signal.

Alex climbs onto the deck above the chart room with his copper-green sextant, sits on the boom and leans into the sagging canvas sail. Elsa, poised at the cabin door with pencil and paper, is ready to take the data as Alex gives it.

Squinting into the eyepiece of the sextant, Alex "pulls" the sun down to the horizon using the instrument's split mirror. After a minute's waiting for the right moment he shouts to Elsa, "Now!" She checks the time and waits for Alex to turn the corroded instrument on its side to read the angle he has just measured. "It's thirty-six degrees, fourteen minutes."

"Thirty-six degrees, fourteen minutes," echoes Elsa, recording the reading.

"Once more. Ready . . . NOW! Oh, a good sight, Elsa!" He again reads the sextant and she writes down the figure. One more time just to be sure, and she descends into the chart room to work out the fix. Booming and beeping cease. Quietness closes in, and in the rocking silence of the chart room she uses pencil and paper to calculate our position. Again, how different the ways of navigation. Instrument navigation is discontinuous, and we don't know where we are until we have a fix. The wayfinder on the canoe so close to us stays continuously oriented: external verification is neither a possibility nor is it wanted.

Steve informs us in mid-afternoon that this is the first Sunday after the first Full Moon after the vernal equinox. Spring! Some weeks ago Elsa thought ahead to this time, and chocolate Easter eggs appear on this Easter Sunday. And the flatness of the sea today is almost the same as that of a week ago when we were north of the equator and in the doldrums; then she produced the brown bread.

The jenny comes down after a day of limpness. "We're going to rock around this ocean the rest of our lives"; and we know of Lee Kyselka's impatience. The sharp interface of sea and sky is everywhere around. A vapid view. It seems that the heat and evaporation near the equator should produce clouds. Not so: it's a dull and lifeless scene.

Nainoa reports:

Right now the wind is going in circles. It's light, slowly spinning the canoe. I have no idea why it's so calm. I'd like to see this on satellite photo. I think it's all kind of neat, for we've run into everything on this trip—every weather condition short of a hurricane. But it *should* be this way because we all signed on the canoe to learn.

It's hard to get the days together. Wind, speed of the canoe, direction—they're all so variable. The wind is really warm, like our warm *kona* winds at

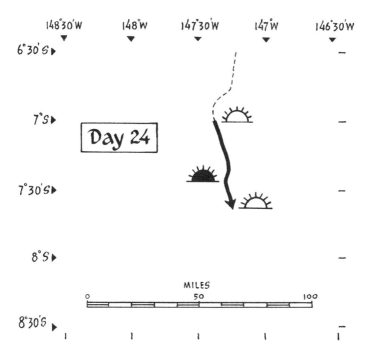

home. Lucky we're heading straight south so we can get out of this. If we stay here a week I've got to change my course plan and add in the current. As we sit here we're moving to the west about 16 miles a day.

I think we're on the line. We're two current days to the west, so we're already on the line. And every day we stay here and don't move, we move one house to the west in the current. All these variables—I've got to get home and figure it all out. It's demanding when it gets hot here, real hot. I have a hard time concentrating when it gets so hot. My head gets heavy from the heat.

Surrounding us this morning of our 24th day at sea are towering cumulus clouds with dark squalls beneath. We watch the clouds billowing upward in convection cells, seeming to turn inside out. A slight breeze comes up as we head toward a squall and for a possible trickle of rain.

"Cloud cover feels good after that long exposure to the sun," says Lee aboard *Ishka*. "When the jenny stops flapping and just hangs there, all I can hear is the faint rustle of water against *Ishka*'s hull as it breaks the flatness of the surface. A few birds are flying around us, more than we have been seeing. Still we're a long way from land.

It's 250 miles southwest to Caroline Island and nearly twice that to the Marquesas. Look! One bird just caught a fish. Anything that moves in this lifeless place is interesting.''

Steve gives us some facts and expresses a concern: ''*Hōkūleʻa* has used an average of 6.87 gallons of water a day during its first two weeks of sailing. But now in this hot weather the consumption has gone up to 9.33 gallons per day. We've allowed a half-gallon per person per day—7 gallons per day for the entire crew. We started with enough water for thirty-two days. However, the increased consumption of water brings us a survival problem. The situation is not crucial at this time, only uncomfortable.''

''No southeast swell today,'' reports Nainoa;

that's scary because it means that the southeast wind that we're counting on is not there. That big ʻĀkau roller must be coming all the way from Hawaiʻi.

We're two days behind schedule. That means we've been in the west current for two extra days. I'm adding it onto the reference course. If we had been here two days ago, we would be three days east of the line. So I add in the current and subtract two westing days from the reference course. If we stop dead in the water tomorrow, we should be one sailing day forward by my account, adding one day to the west. But now I'm also having to consider the amount of water left as well as the time we might be at sea, and where the land lies.

Wind is still light on the morning of our 25th day at sea. The problem is how to deal with such an unusual, unexpected, and so prolonged a situation. One way is to philosophize.

''We're here because that's where we want to be,'' says Mike. Alex picks up that theme with, ''It's bound to change.'' And, sensing the profound historic and scientific importance of this moment he adds, ''This voyage belongs to the ancients.''

A 5-foot brown shark follows *Ishka*. We toss it a little bit of canned meat which it gently sniffs out and gracefully takes into its mouth. Over the next day we grow quite fond of our companion, looking each time we go on deck to see if it is still with us.

Mugginess is upon us. Anticipation and actuality are not here congruent. Cloud cover is 100 percent. No wind at all. Alex pleads for patience, ''Old Polynesians would never have complained of this.''

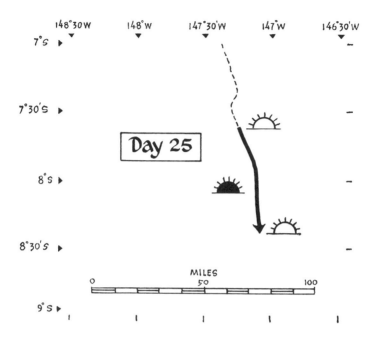

Is the slow speed of the heavy escort vessel an albatross around Nainoa's neck, a detriment to his years of training and discipline? Gordon begins searching for alternatives to tricing up and waiting for *Ishka*. He feels that Nainoa might be under unusual duress in this becalmed sea and wonders if navigation is in jeopardy since it is based on the canoe's moving, not sitting. Steve asks Nainoa how much of a handicap it is.

Nainoa: That's hard to say. I would imagine that we might be 50 miles ahead of where we are, maybe more like 30. Add up all the hours and I'll bet it would be only something like 15 hours.

Steve: I know that some of those times we were doing only one knot ourselves, sometimes 3.

Nainoa: I'd say that we might have averaged 2.5 knots, so like maybe 35 miles of waiting. That's nothing. It's only psychological. Really what we both need is wind.

The sound of an airplane! Right out of the mid-afternoon sun at 5,000 feet appears a four-engine Navy plane, a starboard propeller feathered to minimize fuel consumption.

"There they are!" Three Polynesian Voyaging Society members—Bernie Kilonsky, John Carlmark, and Dixon Stroup—are in that plane doing their research. Their project is that of measuring ocean temperatures at various depths in the sea between Hawai'i and Tahiti by dropping thermometers and recording data as the instruments sink to a depth of a thousand feet. The result of this study may be a more accurate way of predicting weather patterns on the west coast of the Americas. Certainly it may provide a way of better understanding the El Niño condition that occurs when the normal trade wind flow weakens and warm surface water begins flooding eastward out of the western Pacific.

What an unusual sound, the whir of airplane engines on a soundless sea! The C-130 banks and swoops low in a figure-8 around the two vessels. Finding us means that they're getting satellite fixes from the transponder aboard *Hōkūle'a*. Only such data could make possible their pinpointing us so accurately.

They climb back up into the sky, waggle their wings, and disappear into the sun from whence they came. The outside world has come to us at a good time. We return to our quietness and to a very red sunset.

Mirroring that very red sunset is sunrise on our 26th day at sea. Same clouds, same colors, same stillness.

This is our slowest day. John, at the wheel of *Ishka,* talks of South America, Australia, the southwest American desert, of snakes, bluegrass music, of Santa Fe, pottery—just about anything he can think of as we creep along all day at one knot.

Hōkūle'a seems to be moving too rapidly, too soon, too much to the west. Surely they'll miss Tahiti. The south equatorial current is taking us toward the west. To make matters worse, they seem to be steering southwest. We cannot tell them, of course, and all we can do is watch and deal with our own anxiety.

Rain clouds and lightning are ahead of us, and Steve reports: "We're heading south very, very slowly. Nainoa is of the opinion that a weather system in the direction of the rising moon may have been blocking the normal flow of south trade winds. The crew is anticipating rain, but Mau indicates that wind, not rain, will be coming from the lightning."

The shortwave radio again beeps and booms, "It is now 1717

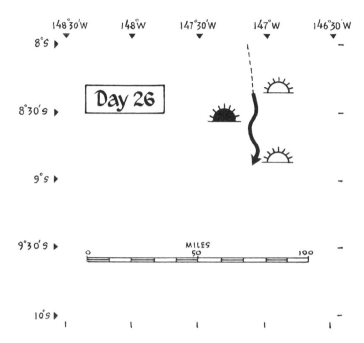

Coordinated Universal Time." Alex with sextant and Elsa with notebook swing into action for a Wednesday morning line of position. A week ago we all were so certain that we'd be swinging into action this Friday night at a disco in Pape'ete. Today we have no idea when we'll reach Tahiti—if ever.

Our friendly brown shark has been replaced by a group of jumping and snorting porpoises. When they leave we're left in stillness. Alex speaks to us of patience, opens the deck cover, and descends into the bilge to work on the engines.

Our slowest day at sea blends into an equally placid night with Venus casting a beam onto the glassy sea. Close to Venus is Makali'i, the "cluster of little eyes."

Binoculars resolve a fuzzy path of light in the southern heavens into the famous Omega Centauri cluster, a globular cluster of a hundred thousand very old stars bound by gravity into spherical shape. A study of this and other globulars fifty years ago led astronomers to conclude that the sun is not at the center of the Milky Way galaxy but in a spiral arm some 30,000 light years from the galactic nucleus.

Steve: I don't know why we're whispering, Nainoa, but what about the winds and swells?

Nainoa: The wind is 5 knots maximum from 'Ākau—just a whisper from the north. The swell is from ENE Manu, a big, clear, long swell. There's also one from the north. But there's no wind at all, just rising air.

Steve: This is our 26th day out of Hilo, right? And our 20th current day from the beginning of navigation, right?

Nainoa: Right. Twenty west-current days, three east-current days. We subtract three of those from twenty to give us seventeen west-sailing days.

Steve: What other navigational thoughts do you have?

Nainoa: We have the problem of water. If we had lots of water we'd go straight south, but we're going west because we're running low. I figured we'd have the trades here but we're not getting them. We're waiting for the wind.

The serenity of the tropical night is shattered in the early morning hours by a fireball whizzing into the earth's atmosphere.

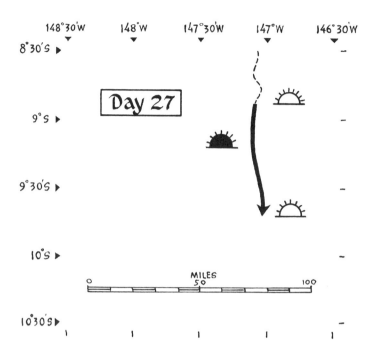

"I was settled back on the bench in the cockpit of *Ishka* looking up at the stars," says Lee at sunrise on our 27th day at sea.

It was about two in the morning. The Southern Cross was swinging back and forth as the boat rocked. Alpha and Beta Centauri were beautifully high and bright.

Suddenly there it was—a bright yellow ball of fire with a tail 5° to 10° long. I moved fast and shook John who was at the wheel. My demanding scream startled him and we both watched it, whatever it was, moving down at a steep angle. It seemed to pause about 10° above the horizon, then disintegrate in a flash. By that time its tail had shrunken to a third of its initial length. I was more excited than scared. I feel so fortunate to have seen it—and it happened so fast, in about ten seconds.

High cirrus clouds are putting a lid on the rising columns of warm air this morning, forcing the air sideways into mushroom shapes. Winds die and the sea regains its glassiness. Sails droop, and Nainoa describes the condition:"We should call this the see-that-feel-that place. Or the one-hull-the-other-hull place . . . or the forward-backward-sideways place. We're turning and rocking and sitting in all directions.''

Sam Ka'ai talks with Steve about his fishhook experiment:

The hook is called *makaukaiwi,* meaning 'bone hook.' It is a double-pieced *ulua* hook where barb and shank are lashed at the base of the curve. The shank itself is lashed to a cord. No knots are involved. Many fine threads bind it together.

I have prepared numerous traditional fishhooks of bone, *ka iwi,* and the mother-of-pearl shell, *pā mele,* including the *pā* style trolling hooks, as well as the two-piece *ulua makau* style hook with feathers.

By using these native style hooks we're gathering information on the types of fish caught with each hook. We're also identifying the birds in the area where strikes are made, and we'll document the landing of the fish.

I believe that this is another way to educate our young people, to bring them closer to living Hawaiian culture, to kindle the spirit of relating past and present to the future. We hope to be able to make a statement about the effectiveness of ancient style hooks, a statement that will contribute to the pride of Hawai'i today.

We travel 45 miles from sunrise to sunrise. That's a distance of less than a half sailing day in one full day of travel—a slight improvement over yesterday's 30 miles. At sunrise on the 28th day we're $9.5°$ S and beginning to pick up a little wind. Nainoa does his mathematics:

When we were one sailing day south of the equator, we were five houses above the line. Then we traveled three more days west of the line. That put us two houses west of the line, not counting current. Adding in the current gives us four more houses west. That's a total of six houses west of the line right now. We have five more houses to lose before we reach Tahiti.

My strategy is to stay on this course. If we can make the Tuamotus, it will be Mataiva Island. If we do it in six days going south, we lose three sailing days, plus another four days of sailing to the west. Technically we should miss Mataiva, but we'll go on this course anyway. I still feel confident that we are east of the line because I've been conservative throughout this whole trip. We'll just stay on Hema for the next six days and try to make the Tuamotus.

Land is getting near. Today *Hōkūle'a* reports a black noddy tern, or *noio.* Yesterday it was a leaf, and three days ago a *koa'e kea* bird.

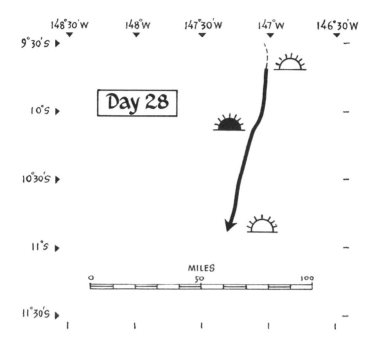

"We saw a squall approaching this afternoon," reports Steve on the evening schedule, "and hoped to be able to catch some water from it. We laid out the canvas, plastic sheets, buckets, and water jugs. It rained, just enough to wet the skin and give a pleasant relief to the hot day but there was nothing to catch. The 30 gallons previously caught are being used in the galley. As of today we have 79 gallons of fresh water in stock."

We pass the 10° S latitude line at sunset and travel through the night at a speed of 4 knots. In the darkness before dawn Nainoa has several clues to latitude: "The pair star in the Obtuse Triangle gives our latitude as 11° S. Using the 15° star and Dubhe, we get 12°. The 23° star and Merak give us 12°. Phecda gives 12° with the 22° hand span. Alioth measures 11.5° using the hand span. The 20° star gives 12° with my four fingers open. Measuring with Kochab, the 18° star and the 24° star all average out to 11° S."

Seas are splashing against the vessels for the first time in ages. How good to see white caps again! "First land in three or four days. Or if we see no land at all then, Tahiti in six days."

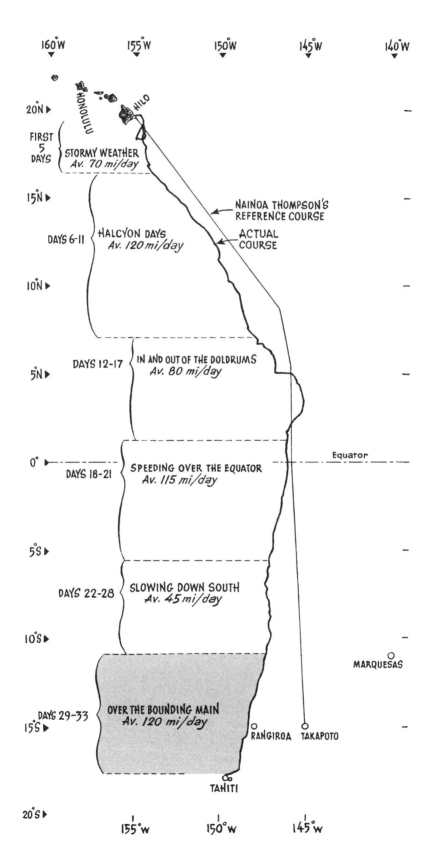

The Bounding Main

"*G*ood smoke" beneath the clouds on this morning of our 29th day at sea indicates good surface winds. Trade winds are wedging in under the high clouds. Mixing in this shear zone is affecting the buildup of clouds. As a result, the towering cumuli are not so towering any more.

"Request both vessels sail in close company tomorrow night," radios Gordon. "A 24-hour lookout will be posted. Request any information on safety or possible peril be given directly to the captain."

Buddy McGuire talks with Steve: "I got interested in *Hōkūleʻa* after talking with Makaʻala Yates who had made the 1976 return voyage as well as the Kealaikahiki trip. I was on the 1978 voyage."

Steve: You're a gourmet cook aboard *Hōkūleʻa*.

Buddy: I spend lots of time cleaning and cutting fish. I used to do it at the Willows restaurant, and that's the way I cut fillets aboard this canoe. All you have to do is look at me and know I love to eat.

Steve: What do you see as the purpose of this trip?

Buddy: We're a support group for documenting the navigational experience of Nainoa. But some of my own desires and whims are also being fulfilled.

Steve: And what might they be?

Buddy: Sailing the South Pacific. I've dreamed of it since I was a child. I had a couple of chances but I thought I'd better finish school. So I never did. Then I got in the service and got married. All these things precluded the possibility of making an ocean trip before this time.

Steve: About the fishing—we caught about nineteen so far including that little prehistoric jobbie. What kind are we catching?

191

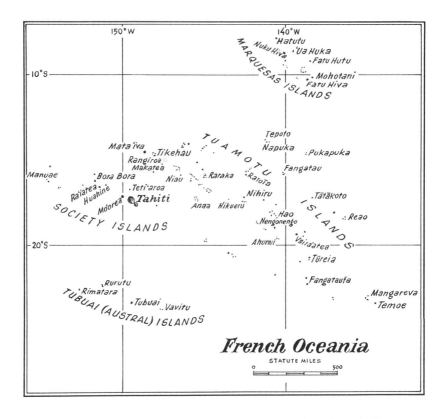

Buddy: *Mahimahi, aku, ono*—with *aku* having the edge I believe.
Steve: Given the rigs we have and the ones that have been broken, how big were the big ones?
Buddy: Forty pounds, easy.
Steve: Those are the ones that just snap and make a loud bang. You know almost without looking that the lure is gone.
Buddy: *Ahi* are notorious for cutting lines.
Steve: What are the highlights of this trip for you?
Buddy: Several. For one, I'm amazed at the skill of Mau and Tava. When we had problems with the boom, I was fascinated in watching Mau repair it in the middle of the night using an adz. It is the most beautiful scarf job and lashing I've ever seen. Incredible! Later he made a miniature of a Satawal sailing canoe. Here he is with his foot resting on a block of wood, his thumb an inch away from the adz, and he's on the weaving and rolling deck of *Hōkūle‘a*, just chipping

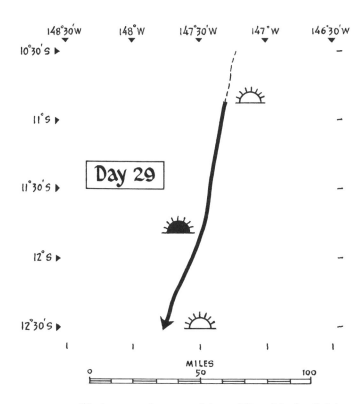

away with immaculate precision. That kind of thing really jazzes me.

Steve: And Tava?

Buddy: Tava is very natural about everything he does. One night he was up on the forward *manu* with his harpoon, and he actually speared a small *mahimahi* right through the center. I appreciate talent. That's talent.

Steve: What have you learned from this trip? Like what skills or new things?

Buddy: Patience.

Steve: Anything else?

Buddy: Lots about lashing and knots—tying knots, back ties, lock knots, whatnots. Lots about sailing. More awareness. I think that it's all part of a contemplative process that this trip has brought about.

During the night Nainoa uses the Obtuse Triangle for latitude, as well as Merak, Dubhe, Phecda, Megrez, and Alioth. "They all show that we're a little more than 13° south. Tomorrow we'll be nine houses west of the line and near Mataiva. If we don't see land by 18° south we'll tack back to find Tahiti."

Steve: The other night you mentioned that you had used some-
          thing like only a fifth of the stars you knew.
Nainoa: That was for direction. Latitude—I use them all.

Land is near. Birds are becoming increasingly evident, and Nainoa reports: "The *manu kū* is the main homing bird. It flies out a hundred miles. In closer, you look for the *noio,* or noddy tern with the white head. It sleeps on the land and doesn't go out as far as *manu kū.* Look for the birds tomorrow morning, for sure in the afternoon. Maybe we'll see land then or at night; for sure the following morning. We'll turn Hema at sunrise to get maximum southing during the day. We have a better chance of seeing the land in daylight hours."

Just after sunrise on our 30th day at sea we see a *manu kū.* "If we don't see land today, tonight, or tomorrow night, then I think we're too far to the west. But the signs are good. I don't see the southeast swell, probably because it's blocked by the Tuamotu chain. The water looks pretty *malie* [calm, quiet, still]. I saw some black birds but that really doesn't mean a thing until they group. Look for the noddy tern with the white head. Today could be the day."

Again we use a floating object alongside *Ishka* to calculate our speed—4.7 knots. "We're galloping!" says Alex in a burst of enthusiasm. That's five times the speed we were making a few days ago, a speed that will carry us 120 miles this sailing day. But why is speed so important? For some reason it is. Birds wheel about in the sky, busy at their work while Alex sings at the wheel.

Nainoa thinks Mau's knowledge of the birds is uncanny: "He uses only two or three. That's all he needs; they guide him to the land. We don't know exactly where land is, but if we see birds going in a certain direction, then we'll go for it." At sunset Steve reports a land bird flying in the same direction that *Hōkūle'a* is traveling, meaning of course that land lies directly ahead.

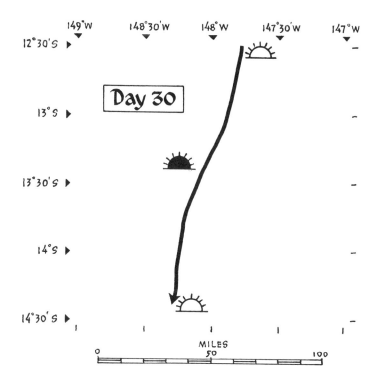

"We're *pau* [finished] the course," says Nainoa. "Now we search for land. It's near." Most of the voyage is concerned with wayfinding and direction keeping. Now that land is near, *landfinding* is the task and the clues are different from those in the open ocean.

Hōkūleʻa follows the bird into the twilight. Aboard *Ishka* we know that there's no possibility of running up on a coral island this night. But those aboard *Hōkūleʻa* do not know. They must be tense and apprehensive, traveling so fast in the darkness of a New Moon toward land that is so near.

"Actually there's a surprising amount of light around us just from the stars," reports Steve on VHF. He continues:

Tava and Chad are our special watch-keepers forward. They cling to the rigging and peer ahead into the darkness. There's a wonderful anticipation as we come toward land. We're at the latitude of the Tuamotus. Where will we make landfall? The Tuamotu Archipelago is long, stretching 1,200 miles to the southeast.

The complexion of the trip changes as we anticipate landfall. We look for lights and listen for the sound of surf. Jo-Anne stands behind Chad and Tava near the secondary line of the Laehu sail. Pat is keeping watch on the starboard side of the galley area. Nainoa is at the stern, clinging to a shroud line on the Lahope mast. Gordon stands behind him. Buddy and Leon finish cleaning the galley, then join Mau, Shorty, Marion, and Sam in searching for land on the port side. Forward of the stern net is Harry Ho, looking backward and keeping an eye on *Ishka* as he looks for land.

It's about four in the morning. Maui's Fishhook lies ahead of us high above the Laehu sail. The mast seems to be pointing directly toward the center of our galaxy. Aquarius is rising and Corvus is setting. We're sailing 6 or 7 knots in the southeast trades. Occasional waves break against the windward hull, dousing those on deck.

At sunrise on our 31st day *Hōkūle‘a* is hove-to, waiting and watching for birds. No birds. Sea, sky, us. *Hōkūle‘a* hoists sails and takes off. The horizon is clear in the east but it's cloudy overhead. Aboard *Ishka* we're out of cooking oil and use mayonnaise as a substitute. Alex looks at our position on Chart 526 and goes forward to look for land. Mike takes the wheel, leans far over to the port side to get out from under the canopy so that he can see, and the unattended sails flap violently.

"We all realize," says Steve, "that when we make landfall it will never again be the same for this particular group of fourteen persons. Leon is considering the reality of landfall in terms of anchoring or docking. Anchor, ground tackle, chain, swivel, shackle, and line are in their proper places. The tow line is ready. A primary anchor is on the bow, a secondary one at the stern with nearly 300 feet of extra line. Buddy and Pat are responsible for the details in setting the anchors and making sure they hold."

Mid-morning. The signaling mirror of *Hōkūle‘a* is flashing. We turn on the VHF. Leon reports: "Nainoa is at the top of Laehu mast and Shorty is at the top of Lahope. Both see land."

Alex climbs *Ishka*'s mast. Using binoculars, he tentatively identifies the island as Rangiroa. "Congratulations, Gordon," he says on the VHF, "to you and your splendid navigator and to all the crew."

"It's nice to see green," replies Nainoa.

I know the importance of this moment to Nainoa, and my eyes fill with tears. I try talking with him but I'm too clutched up with

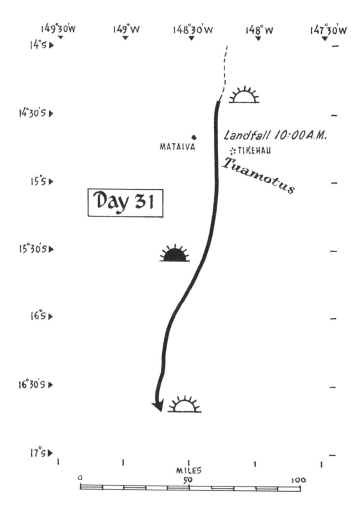

emotion. Someone else takes the microphone. Not only is this landfall the fulfillment of a dream, it's also a closure with Eddie Aikau.

How strange to see, after a month of sharp line of sea and sky, a
forest of spindly coconut trees standing on the horizon! Since coral
islands are so similar in appearance, it takes a few hours to make positive identification. It turns out that this is Tikehau, not Rangiroa.
Tikehau is one island east of Mataiva where *Hōkūleʻa* made landfall
in 1976.

We sail between Tikehau and Mataiva, flying the flags of the
United States, the state of Hawaiʻi, France, and Tahiti. We're only a

Marion Lyman

few miles from Mataiva but we cannot see it in the glare of the after-noon sun. And, in reflections of another sort, we realize that it was also on its 31st day four years ago that *Hōkūle‘a* made landfall on that island now in the sun, Mataiva. Of interest, too, although in no way related to this trip, is that we're only 200 miles west of Raroīa Island upon which *Kon Tiki* crashed after a voyage lasting more than three times longer than ours.

Far ahead is the faint, rounded form of Makatea Island, growing slowly in size as we move toward it. We watch it disappearing in the dusk as we enjoy a sunset dinner. And later, in the darkness, Venus again casts its beams upon the waves.

Marion tells Steve of her feelings:

Today was a very melancholy day for me. Virtually our whole port side forward was filled with low islands, sandy patches, and palm trees swaying in the trade winds. I had a strong vision of Eddie Aikau and his smiling face. I imagined him here, probably running around the deck and asking Sam if he could blow the conch shell. I also deeply miss my big brother, Dave, who would have enjoyed sighting land and experiencing all that we have shared on this trip.

A high point each day on the trip for me was the evening time when we'd gather on the afterdeck. The sun had cooled off and we all had more energy. Dinner over, dishes washed, stomachs filled, and we would talk in the twilight. A friendliness there was at that time, a harmony of the crew with people staying awake to share time with those on the other watch.

Another highlight was with Mau and Tava. We were on the afterdeck one time munching on coconut. Mau started asking me about my experience in the Peace Corps in Palau, an island in the Caroline Islands group 600 miles west of his island of Satawal. We three sat there, eating dried fish and coconut. Very genuine people both Mau and Tava, and that was a very special moment for me.

Makatea is well behind us as the sun rises on our 32nd day at sea. Tahiti lies far over the horizon but we want to see it now. Here's where we need all the patience we can summon, for we're still in the open ocean, 150 miles from Tahiti. The journey is over but we haven't yet arrived. Landfall and destination—Tikehau and Tahiti—are two days apart. Patience!

"Radio Mahina, this is *Ishka*. Request instructions on entering Pape'ete Harbor."

Since welcoming ceremonies (one at the high commissioner's house and one with the mayor) are set for tomorrow, we receive the message: "Do not enter the pass before 0730 hours tomorrow morning. Two big vessels are entering the harbor, one at 0530 hours and the other at 0630 hours."

Steve: What do you think of the trip, Mau?

Mau: This trip good. Everything good.

Steve: How do you feel personally? You feel good being on the voyage?

Mau: Yah, happy. I feel good.

Steve: How about the navigation? You think Nainoa did a good job?

Mau: Yah, Nainoa is better. I go with them on the trip to watch Nainoa. Now Nainoa is everything good.

Steve: In your thinking, are there some ways Nainoa can improve?

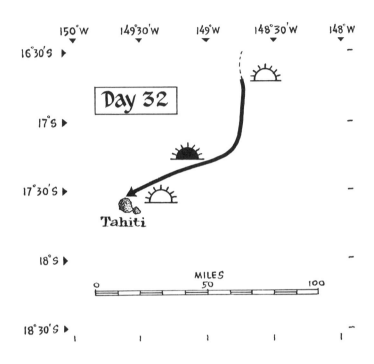

Mau: Yah. Nainoa I think no problem for him after the trip. Maybe he like make another after this sometime. He like make another one—good. No problem.

Steve: How do you like *Hōkūle'a* compared to other vessels you've been on?

Mau: Oh, yah. Good.

Steve: We've had our problems. But of course you certainly helped us out, like fixing the boom and what not. Is that pretty much what you have to expect, sometimes problems with boats at sea? And you just have to be ready to deal with it?

Mau: Yah.

Steve: Have you, in fact, been on other boats or sailing canoes where things have broken and then you've had to fix them while at sea?

Mau: Say what?

Steve: Things that have broken or gone wrong, so to speak. I'm wondering if at other times that you have sailed, if other things have broken, like another broken boom or torn sail—any of these things ever happen to you?

Mau: Before? Oh yah.

Steve: And then you had to just deal with it, like mend the sail, fix the boom. What kinds of things have happened, Mau?

Mau: On my canoe? My canoe turn over two times and I turn it back again in the ocean.

Steve: Was it in a storm of strong wind?

Mau: Yah. Storm. Storm almost just like typhoon. Boom go broke. But people from my island know about any kind stuff make on the canoe and everybody fix anything go broke on trip. Everybody fix.

We keep well east of Tahiti, upwind, to avoid the small island of Teti'aroa. Darkness has fallen by the time the anchors are set, and we rest outside Pape'ete Harbor. This is our night of two Venuses—one, the brilliant planet setting behind the island of Mo'orea; the other, the brilliant flashing beam of the lighthouse on Point Venus on Tahiti.

Point Venus derives its name from an important scientific expedition led by Captain James Cook. He anchored in Matavai Bay in 1769 to observe Venus crossing the face of the sun. A "transit of Venus" is a rare event, important to astronomers. It happens less often than once a century. And then the transit occurs twice in an interval of eight years. The 1761 transit showed Venus to have an atmosphere. The observation of the 1769 transit was used to determine the earth's distance from the sun. At that time solar distance was known to within an accuracy of only 30 percent.

Sir Edmund Halley (a comet bears his name) suggested that if observations of the transit were made from widely scattered places on earth, that uncertainty might be reduced to less than one percent. The concept was sound, even though the results of that first world-wide coordinated scientific endeavor were not as definitive as had been hoped. The next transit pair of Venus will be in the years 2004 and 2012.

Charles Darwin landed at Matavai Bay in 1835. Like Cook before him, he was greeted by a crowd of happy, laughing men, women, and children. Delighted with the response he called it "charming Tahiti." Then he sailed on to New Zealand, and in that vast stretch of sea he wrote in masterful understatement, "It is necessary to sail over this great ocean to comprehend its immensity."

Our 33rd day at sea, and the rays of the rising sun touch the jagged 7,171-foot summit of Tahiti's highly eroded shield volcano, Mt. Orohena. Looming out of the morning mist to the west and veiled in clouds is the island of Moʻorea.

As we proceed toward the harbor of Papeʻete, the sound of drum and conch shell grow louder. We're ready for a Tahiti welcome and Steve captures the moment in three interviews.

Steve: What's your feeling right now, Chad?
Chad: Almost tearful. Tearful. It's been such a great experience. I just love everybody. I think we are history now; we're reestablishing a tradition that used to be. We're all a part of it.
Steve: All right, Chad. Thanks. And what's your feeling now, Marion?
Marion: Mixed, happy. No, I wouldn't say mixed. It's all good, all positive, all happy. It's been beautiful. The dream is over and it's time to get back to the business of living.

Steve: Thanks, Marion. And as we enter Pape'ete Harbor, Captain Pi'ianai'a, what is your feeling?

Gordon: What feeling? Is this Pape'ete? I thought it was Mataiva.

We clear "the pass" at exactly 0730 hours. Outriggers swarm around *Hōkūle'a* and escort her into the center of Pape'ete Harbor to the welcoming crowd of several thousand persons. A man on a solitary tug tosses a line and tows *Ishka* to a berth at the east end of the town. We secure the sloop and walk a brisk mile on solid ground to festivities that are, by now, well underway.

Pat Aiu describes the welcoming scene in his journal:

At least a dozen light planes flew overhead, banking into tight turns for a better view. And the canoes—single ones, double ones, long ones, small ones, sailing types, paddling types, and one with an outboard motor—all jockeyed around *Hōkūle'a* for position and a better look, and to come in close to touch her sides. In Tahiti and the surrounding archipelago, canoe racing, paddling and sailing are at the top in sporting activity, an integral part of their life style.

Love, respect, and awe of *Hōkūle'a* just radiated from the eyes of the people. And she was graceful today. I was on the steering sweep during entry and she responded like a ballerina—no wallowing or slipping. She just glided gracefully up to her mooring buoy on the beach. The beach, for perhaps a half-mile, was packed with people wanting to see *la pirogue Hōkūle'a*, and with little children wanting to come closer to see and to touch the canoe.

After the formal greeting by the mayor of Pape'ete, we walked down the main street a few blocks to the governor's mansion. The gendarmes couldn't hold the crowd any longer. The crew was separated as the crowd surged around individuals to say, "*I ora na*. Hello. Welcome to Tahiti. Aloha," presenting us leis and kissing us on both cheeks.

The Wayfinder

What goes on in the mind of the wayfinder? We've had glimpses of what goes on in Nainoa's mind in his interviews with Steve. Here, in this chapter, he tells us what it is like to spend a month continuously attentive to the task of finding land. We are also given a glimpse of the dreadful loneliness that attends risk and the fulfillment in competent performance.

The account in this chapter is of the 1980 return voyage from Tahiti to Hawai'i. The words are Nainoa's, the form is mine. The words come from tape recordings, talk-story times, and a paper he submitted in English 101. Much of the original is reflexive—Nainoa recalling, remembering, relating, piecing together, thinking in retrospect what the experience must have been at the time. To preserve the immediacy of events, I've put it all into present tense.

*I*t seems to me that the way I shivered at night in the cold aboard *Hōkūle'a* in the storm after we left Hilo was the same as when I was young and diving at night along the reef. The wind and the ocean supply the cold, and I understand nature through exposure to it. I cannot really convey the feeling within me of that wind any more than I can tell you what it is like being the navigator. Yet that is my task in this chapter.

May 13, 1980

Sunrise on the cliffs of Matavai Bay at Point Venus. Each morning for five days we've been watching for the wind. But, just as on our departure from Hawai'i, the wind has not yet been ready to grace the sails and allow *Hōkūle'a* to glide along sea roads traveled by explorers of old. We've been waiting for a straight wind, a wind to depart on. Today we have that wind. It's not an ideal wind but it is one that we'll depart on.

The canoe is ready for the sea. A new boom replaces the one we broke on the trip down. Stress had also caused the laminations on the crossbeams to begin separating. Metal plates were bolted to them to strengthen them for the return trip.

It's late afternoon when we depart Tahiti. A ceremony once again affirms the bond between Polynesian peoples and sends us on our way. The setting sun is casting its last rays on high clouds as we leave Tahiti behind in SW Na Leo. Soon the first stars appear and the heavens demand our attention. Thoughts of the hospitality of our Tahitian friends and family are put away and we are left with only ourselves and our memories.

The Southern Cross is now high in the sky behind us. Each night for the next three or four weeks we'll see it slightly lower, and by the time we reach Hawai'i it will be at the horizon. It will be ten days yet before we'll see the North Star. During the next few hours the tiny island of Teti'aroa will be moving along our star compass from 'Ākau to Hema as we pass close to it.

The first dawning of light is the important time for the navigator. It is the time for judging the sea and swells relative to the positions of the stars, a time for the reading of the weather for the day. Light creates the day and the colors in the clouds and in the mists in the salt air. Mau has internalized countless sunrises, so he knows how to read the weather and when it is right to sail. For him this knowledge is the means of survival of his island's people. For us this canoe is our way of understanding the people of old.

Navigating without instruments is a personal act. You must know the principles but you cannot reduce wayfinding to a set of formal operations. I'm constantly discovering new things that are useful in getting the canoe there.

On this trip I've been getting glimpses of a greater world of navigation, far beyond what I prepared myself for. I learn through my culture, but that alone is not enough: it does not provide all the right answers. When I understand things without knowing how, that's when I know I've taken great steps.

Like knowing where the moon is: One night it was really cloudy.

It was nearly a Full Moon but clouds were so thick you couldn't see it. Still I knew where it was even though there was no reason for me to know. I could have figured it out analytically, but I already knew. Here's a separation between knowledge and understanding. At times like that I know, but I don't know how I know.

Sleep is not a problem. I thought it might be but it isn't. When you accept responsibility internally you don't need all that much sleep. In a way you've got no choice. You make the decision to be here, and once you're here you're accountable.

Mau says he never sleeps when he's navigating. He says his eyes are closed but inside he's not. Somehow he rests enough to take care of the fatigue and he maintains his orientation. It's fascinating, this man's abilities.

My job is getting the canoe there, not to find out what ancient people did. That understanding comes as a result of a task gladly accepted. This is a unique situation—being responsible for giving direction and getting the canoe there without ever having done it before. It's full of unknowns.

There's a world out here that I didn't know anything about until forced into it by my choices. Analytic thinking alone cannot bring understanding, and I'm glad of that. We aren't searching for understanding, but understanding is coming as a result of the search.

In a sense there were no choices once we got into certain situations. That won't be reflected in the transcripts because at the time it happens I cannot express how I know. I don't understand at the time, and I still cannot express it. The transcripts are pictures of the struggle I feel at a particular moment.

FINDING THE LAND

June 1, 1980

Dawn. The first rays of dawn hurt my eyes after straining all night to maintain the sailing course. I have an uneasy feeling this morning, for I know that the thin sheetlike layer of cirrus cloud that moved in last night can mean a change in the weather—a change from the regular trades—and that can make navigating difficult. It was difficult last night, at times impossible, even to identify the stars that did show through the breaks. This morning the cloud is too high and

too thin to cause shadows, but it makes the sea look more gray than blue.

The soreness in my eyes at dawn comes from the strain and fatigue of keeping *Hōkūle'a* on course. Most of the night we steered by the moon. It is now two days past Full Moon phase, the night of the month that Hawaiians call Lā'au Kū Kahi. Fortunately for us it was a big moon, nearly opposite the sun, and its light was with us most of the night. When it is nearly round and close to the horizon we use it for steering.

The sun rose this morning in the house of ʻĀina on the star compass. It is most reassuring (and a compliment to the crew) to find both the canoe and the rising sun in their correct positions. For myself and the crew who had the steering duty for the last four hours, relaxation is now in order as the sun comes up.

With the sun on the horizon we have a solid steering sign. It's in the house of ʻĀina, so we can assume that we sailed a most accurate course during the starless night. I feel the urge to give in to my fatigue, but it is not yet time to sleep.

The steering swells in line with the sun are clearer and more defined than they were yesterday. Each day since we left the doldrums the swells have been getting more and more defined, sorting themselves out in the dominant trade winds.

Daylight hours. I cannot relax on this first day of June. Because of the persistent high cloudiness, we have not seen stars very much in the last ten days. We're going 6.5 knots, but I do not have the vital information needed on our position change. I cannot relax. That's the hardest part for me, both mentally and physically. The conflict in mind and body brings tenseness and fatigue at a time I most need to be alert.

I estimate that we have traveled 260 miles without positioning ourselves by the stars. That's an empty feeling as we approach the target of the Hawaiian Islands.

We steer most of the day off the wind. Since morning the wind has shifted to east northeast, a change that brings a familiar coolness that reminds me of the normal trade winds of Hawaiʻi. I have pondered many times the familiarness of new experiences during the voyage, as if somehow I have had such experiences before. In understanding the blending of my ocean past as a youth with the discipline of sailing lies the most cherished parts of myself.

When the wind swings northeast as it did today, it confuses the swells that we steer by. They lag behind the changing wind direction. For myself, such unsorted swells and waves also leave me confused.

Today we're using the high cloudiness that blocked the stars the last two nights. It's a special circumstance that allows us to use the clouds—very high clouds, moving slowly, very far away. Under these conditions the apparent motion of the canoe will have little effect on the bearing of these nearly stationary clouds.

Sunset. The June sun sets in the house of ʻĀina, two houses north of due west. High clouds in the west around the sun take on a deep red color. The evening is dark, for it is three days beyond Full Moon, and tonight it will rise about three hours after sunset. John Kruse is at the steering sweep, keeping the direction of Na Leo as we sail from day into night. The true wind is right on our beam, and the canoe is quite dry as we race away from the crests of ocean swells.

The air is getting cooler as we increase our distance from the equator. How important the yellow foul-weather gear is to me when I contemplate another night of exposure to wind and waves and rain through ten hours of darkness! So many the reasons to admire the first Polynesian voyagers who sailed without such gear. How natural to be proud of my heritage.

We search the sky this evening for those stars that target the land, but the ocean horizon is clouded over. I have a very unsettled feeling. When we're nearing land we need the stars most—but now they're not there. Instead of getting clues from my eyesight, I'm left to my imagination, and I think of drops of water 10 miles distant blocking the light that has been traveling for 40 years to reach us.

Our course made good all day is between Haka and Na Leo. I estimate that we've traveled 72 miles and that we're 13.5° north of the equator, 7.5 houses west of the course line. I believe the islands of Hawaiʻi to be in the direction of Manu, 550 miles northwest. In the back of my mind, though, I'm bothered by our yesterday's sighting of the *manu kū* [dove]. How can this land bird be so far from land? How can it have flown so far if I'm to believe that it is away from its home island only between dawn and dusk?

June 2, 1980

Dawn. Since sunset last night I estimate we sailed 60 to 70 miles north northwest. A few stars of the land showed in the middle of the night through gaps in the cloudy sky indicating that we are 14° north of the equator.

The eastern horizon is showing a lot of red as sunrise approaches. High cirrus clouds are still present, with cumulus clouds at low levels showing the surface trade winds. Bruce takes command of the steering sweep as we enter the most critical phase of the voyage— targeting the Hawaiian Islands. We have very little room for error.

Nainoa

The sun is replacing night with day. The bearings of the swells are somewhat confusing, apparently because of the changing direction of the wind. Whether it is that way in the sea or just in my mind, I am not sure. I've had little sleep in the last few days. Concentrating is a chore. This is the first time on the voyage, either down or up, that I'm feeling a little sick—a chest cold. Maybe it is anxiety, wondering if we have been accurate with our course. Are the Hawaiian Islands in the direction of northwest 'Āina? Uncertainty occupies my mind. But when forced to make a decision, I know that I have only mind and memory—and faith in myself. Without that I'm lost.

We're doing 6 knots off the wind. Steering is difficult. *Hōkūle'a* is constantly trying to round itself to the windward in an attempt to parallel its hulls with the dominant swells. It takes skill and ability to anticipate the effect of the on-coming swells. Fully loaded, *Hōkūle'a* weighs nearly 10 tons, and that's a lot of weight to control. Once a steersman loses control to the swells there is very little that can be done. Experience is the steersman's greatest teacher.

Daylight. The high clouds disappear and leave the trade wind cumulus, a very good clue to steady trade winds. We have a light lunch, and the crew spends most of the day steering and trimming the sails. Bruce, who is the primary fisherman on this voyage, is constantly tending to the fishing lines. This leg we have been running larger lures than we have run in the past. Even though we have not caught as many fish as we did on the other voyages, those we have hooked have been comparatively big ones. We picked up one nearly 100-pound marlin, a 50-pound sailfish, and a 30-pound *mahimahi*. We also lost at the gaff an *ahi* that I estimated to be 60 pounds. We had our slim share of small *aku, kawakawa*.

Our diet aboard *Hōkūleʻa* is basically canned, packaged, and dried food. All our fresh provisions were eaten, or they were tossed overboard because of spoilage. Last to go were the citrus fruits. A frequent topic of conversation, as we get closer to land, is that of the first things we will eat when we arrive home.

Snake Ah Hee has become our official cook—unofficially. Right from the start of the trip he has taken over in the kitchen. I am certain at times I have seen him fighting over the right to the pots and pans in the galley. Good meals can at times be one of the few things to look forward to at sea, and cooking is not easy at sea on *Hōkūleʻa*.

As the sun nears its setting place on the horizon the canoe is being cleaned. Some of the crew are washing themselves with a salt water bath. Others are putting on their foul-weather gear, preparing for another night at sea. Nathan Wong is steering. Nate sails in the dual role of crew member and physician. Medically we are all healthy and sound. We're grateful for that. We've had our share of minor sunburns and rashes, along with Kainoa Lee's bad cold. It is comforting to have Nate on board in case of a serious problem.

No land birds today. Their absence stirs doubts in my mind. But if my estimate of where we are is correct, we must still be out of the flight range of land birds anyway. It's their absence that makes me uneasy.

Sunset. As the sun sets in the west northwest, I estimate the island of Hawaiʻi to be two houses to the right in the direction of northwest Manu, 360 miles away.

We've traveled, as I estimate it, 72 miles since sunrise in the direction of Na Leo. Winds are 18 knots out of the east northeast as we're sailing 6 knots abeam to the true wind. The wind and swells are steady and straight. With the sky clear of high clouds, it appears we will have good weather at the time we need it most. I feel good about that.

Wedemeyer Au steers *Hōkūle'a* in the direction of the setting sun. In the fading glow of twilight he uses the light of the brighter, very distant stars to guide him as we sail ever toward Hawai'i, our homeland.

The Southern Cross is nearing the southern horizon. Our timing for landfall is critical in that certain groups of stars must be in the right position relative to the sun. The Southern Cross is the most important of the constellations for us now. It is getting toward the west and will be available in its useful position for only a week or ten days more.

As I watch the Southern Cross, so does Mau. He has kept himself uninvolved with the navigation and sailing of *Hōkūle'a*. Navigation takes constant memorization of our course made good. For the most part Mau has divorced himself from that effort; yet as the stars of Hawai'i begin to show in the twilight, anyone with that knowledge cannot help but be concerned about the accuracy of the course we have kept. Are we truly to the east and upwind of Hawai'i?

Steering is easy on this cloudless night, but in the early morning hours I tend to become tired. The more I force myself to stay awake, the more fatigued and less alert I become. I need rest to clear my mind.

We are nearing our destination. Mau scans his ocean heaven for important stars. It is as if I know what he is feeling. I know because of what I have gone through on this voyage. My thoughts are sad as I realize the wealth that he has given me, in sharing navigational secrets in the context of the tradition of his culture. My thoughts are sad that the voyage will soon end and with it his teachings, for he must go back home to Satawal. He is a man of priceless gifts. A man who took our hands, as if we were children, and walked us through it all upon the wake of our ancestors. As I watch him look at the land stars he knows so well, I cannot help but feel sad.

I begin this night full of anticipation, and at the same time I'm very tired. Through this experience I'm beginning to understand the suffering of Mau in maintaining his heritage, a difficult task in a rapidly changing world. I don't know the depth of the hurt he feels in seeing more of his culture lost with each generation.

Night passes with only a partial cloud cover. Stars make their paths across the sky. We're able to use the land stars of the Southern Cross (Hawaiians also know it as Newa), Atria in the Southern Triangle, and the two brilliant stars, Alpha and Beta Centauri. Hōkū-pa'a, the North Star, is gaining altitude each night, and from this array of stars I judge South Point to be 180 miles to the north and 220 miles west of us.

June 3, 1980

Sunrise. Early morning brings a freshening wind of 22 knots from east northeast. I'm cold after another full night of being on the open deck of *Hōkūle'a*. The two bright stars in Aries, Sheratan and Hamal, are rising. At this time of year their appearance on the horizon brings the first light of dawn—a good sign for Snake's watch, which has been on since two this morning. Since we have no timepieces aboard, our simple routines are kept by the light of the stars and sun. The brilliant red and purple colors of these beautiful clouds of dawn, though, may be a sign of bad weather.

Kainoa Lee is steering as the sun breaks the ocean horizon, on this our 21st day at sea. The sun's orange rays are guiding him on his course, northwest Na Leo. With the increased wind speed we are traveling at 8 knots toward the Big Island in the direction of Noio. If we maintain our course and speed, the island should be in 'Āina tonight, not much more than 210 miles away. I feel very uneasy about such estimates: what if we sail more than 200 miles from here and find no land?

Cloud cover is 40 percent, not a comforting thought now that we are so close to land.

I am awakened by loud conversation. I see the sun still near the eastern horizon, and I realize that I have slept only a short while. My mind and body agree. Off the left side of the canoe is a group of white birds. As far as I can tell they're mostly the white tropic bird, *koa'e kea*. But within the group is at least one *manu kū*, the bird that indicates land. The ocean is filled with white caps, so white birds flying low are hard to see. We watch as long as we can see them. Apparently they're fishing, not flying to or from land. Nevertheless, it puts me more at ease in my upcoming sleep to know that we're in the circle of *manu kū* and near Hawai'i.

It's clear to all of us that land is near. We set a watch to keep a sharp lookout for any sign of it. I still feel that we are south and somewhat east of our target, so we hold a course between northwest Na Leo and Nalani. We do not want to sail to the west of the Big Island, so we'll hold that course until we can get a good star clue tonight.

This day seems to pass slower than any other day. We're still straining to see the land. The optimism in seeing land birds in the morning is being tested by the length of the day. In the minds of us all lies the shape of the land.

I was sitting on the aft navigator's platform this afternoon and Steve was sleeping on the forward platform. Suddenly I saw a brown boobie floating on the water about 70 feet off the starboard bow. Just at the moment we were sailing past the resting bird, Steve woke up. He saw it, jumped up and shouted, "Ring-necked mallard! Ring-necked mallard!" I was astonished with his enthusiasm and with that misidentification. I looked at him as he seemed to turn to me to see if he had any reason to think he was correct.

Maybe it was fatigue or merely the absurdity of the situation; anyway I did not even feel the need to react. I just continued studying the ocean as *Hōkūleʻa* sailed past the boobie. Steve straightened himself and collected his wits as if nothing had happened. Had he been right, this "ringed-necked mallard" definitely would have been off-course and in deep trouble. But I guess birds of the land occupy even the dreams of those who sail in search of new islands.

Sunset. We use the last moments of the day to look for birds and any other clues to land.

During the night high clouds move in from the southwest, and on the southern horizon we see the first signs of a build-up of rain squalls—both signs of changing weather. Today was the first day in six that we were able to enjoy relatively clear skies, yet that clarity is now being threatened.

East-northeast winds have heightened to 18 knots. This morning I estimated our distance from land as 210 miles. But almost as if I need to cushion myself from the increasing doubt that is building up in me, just for no reason I changed the distance to the Big Island to 300 miles. Due to my inexperience or immaturity (or both), I changed my thinking to allow the Big Island to be that far away. A

cushion allows for human error and gives us a reason not to panic if we do not see the islands by tomorrow morning.

Rain comes in the early evening twilight. Crew members, now used to the ways of the sea, already have on their foul-weather gear. The clouds are moving with extreme uniformity—distinct cloud streets with rows of cumulus nimbus clouds paralleling each other, equally spaced, and all of the same altitude. Soon the rows of clouds encompass the world of the canoe. As we sail abeam to the wind and rain, we pass from rows of rain to rows of clear sky and on into the night of our 21st day at sea.

Only the stars overhead are visible between the rows of rain. Stars for the land may not show themselves if the rain should stay all night. But let's not think of such things so early in the night with land so close.

As I search for the land in the direction of a particular group of stars, all I see are those rows of rain clouds that we just passed through. But to the east of south I see a break in the clouds, a gap traveling at a speed different from the prevailing trades. I watch and hope it will not change form or continuity, so not to allow the gap to give a clear vision of the stars I seek. As I watch I know the night is very early, and that such stars will be in their correct positions for the land I desire.

The gap in the clouds moves closer to the south. First to appear are the faint stars to the east of what I seek. Moments later, with anticipation, the land stars show themselves in the positions I need them to be. I stare till I'm sure. Now I know by our latitude and dead reckoning that we are close. I turn to my right to see Mau and Mike Tongg staring at the same thing. Nothing is said, for nature has told us all that we need to know.

Most of the night passes with rain. Not until early morning do I see the North Star. The rain makes the sky more clear. Just before the rising moon is Maui's Fishhook (Scorpius) appearing through a break in the clouds. What a magnificent sight, the barb of the Fish-hook in the direction of the center of the Milky Way! High above these clouds and at the top of Mauna Kea, astronomers may right now have telescopes aimed toward that galactic center. A few months ago I was up there in that cold, studying the stars. Thoughts of the old and new blend in my mind.

Anticipation plays tricks with my mind and senses. Not knowing if it's imaginary or real, I struggle with visions of towering mountains appearing above dark rain clouds, much like a child who believes clouds are what things are made of. Continuously I question whether I can feel unusual swell patterns that might be back-wash off the Hāmākua coast. Is that the sound of surf crashing on the cliffs? Rain and cloud are blocking our vision. Such thoughts running through my mind are not based on logic but rather imagination kindled by hope. However, it turns out to be a night only of images that leaves me exhausted. For my own sake I will need to relax. The land will show itself when it will. I must give up and give in to the notion that I can do nothing about it.

June 4, 1980

The first streaks of light on this morning reveal gray and black clouds at both low and high levels. During the night I saw the Southern

Cross near the horizon and I know Hawai'i is near. My experience in seeing Crux from places in Kaua'i, Maui, Kona, and South Point tells me that the canoe is in the latitude of Hawai'i. The time for changing our course from a general northwest direction to a more westerly one is near.

Long rows of low clouds show straight winds coming from NE 'Āina. *Hōkūle'a* is heading NW Na Leo, crosswise to the wind. The rising sun breaks that long dark line into individual puffs of cloud, orange in color. High clouds are becoming more scattered now, showing as thin streaks of red against a background of light blue sky. Straight winds and clearing skies are a welcome sight after the last three days of rain.

A couple of hours before noon we see a thin, gray line beyond a bank of clouds almost dead ahead. With the sun high in the sky and somewhat behind us yet, and with rain clouds lifting, the line seems stationary. It is not particularly distinct. What is it?

We have a meeting of the crew to work out a strategy. We will make two tacks, one at noon and another at sunset. We hope that by holding a course as close as possible downwind we will be able to see for sure if the line that we think we see is an island or not.

Our new tack puts us on a course of SW 'Āina; then I go to sleep for about two hours. When I awake in mid-afternoon, I find we're looking right into the glare of the sun reflecting on the water making the sighting of land in that direction impossible. It also makes it hard to judge the movement of clouds, an important clue in finding land. Clouds over the sea move, but those around the mountains are stationary.

Also steering SW 'Āina after three weeks in NW Na Leo makes the land move differently along the compass. Now the land is moving northward at a speed dependent upon our overall direction and speed during the time I was asleep.

With these two conditions I feel a lack of confidence as to where the line I thought I had seen in the morning really was. Maybe that line had been only in my imagination. We're at the right latitude for Mauna Kea, and now only one question remains: does it lie downwind or upwind, to the west or to the east?

We saw no birds this morning, no sign of *manu kū*. Seeing no birds at all makes the direction of land even more uncertain. Have I been too hasty in turning west to find the land? Could it still lie to the north and my memorizing system be inaccurate? Worst of all, could it be that we are too far to the west, downwind of our destination?

We try steering in the direction of that line we had seen by pointing the canoe almost straight downwind, SW ʻĀina. We have a straight wind from NE ʻĀina and a dominant Hikina swell. Even then, we cannot hold the course. Steering is just too difficult.

I keep straining to see something like images of mountains or clouds that don't move. It's hard to see anything in the glare of this hot afternoon sun. Straining makes me sleepy. I know that. I also know that I'm likely only to be fooling myself. I must be patient and let the mountain show when it is ready.

The plan we had worked out in the morning was to change our tack after dinner so we would not get too far south. Instead, we begin tacking at about 5 P.M. Our new heading is NW ʻĀina, close to the direction of the setting sun. We see no birds at all, making it all the more difficult to know where we are relative to the island of Hawaiʻi.

The sun is nearing the horizon and a peculiar image is forming. I don't know why. The cloud bank turns a dark gray, almost black, like rain. Around the cloud bank, though, is a consistent orange color. It's a strange sight.

Something is different about that setting sun. It's something we haven't seen before. So we alter our course slightly and head directly into the sun, NW ʻĀina.

The crew is silent. I think they have a feeling, too, that land lies just below the sun. It is as if we're all standing on tip-toes waiting, and a feeling comes over me that this is the way things are supposed to be.

I remember a story I was told one time (how accurate I do not know) of the people of ancient Polynesia. They had their family guardians, *kūʻula*, that gave them prosperity. They were symbolized as figures shaped of carved stone. Fishing families had their *kūʻula* that attracted fish and gave them protection. The navigator of old, as the story goes, was not like other men. He was separated from them—a man of the sea, not of the land. So his *kūʻula* was not

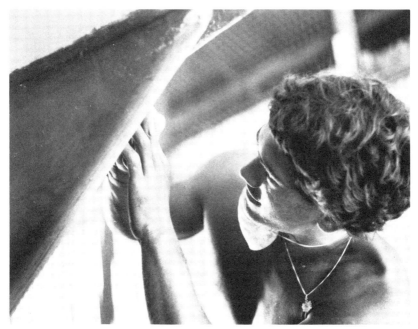

Bruce Blankenfeld

bound to the land but was the land itself—the highest mountain, a mountain of power.

I stand on the bow of *Hōkūleʻa* watching the sun dropping toward that cloud bank and I question how much control, if any, I have in finding the land. This is the way things are supposed to be.

Closer and closer it comes to the cloud, and I have a different, almost strange feeling. The sun is right in the compass direction of ʻĀina—land. It is pointing out the land.

I walk to the bow of the canoe for I know the island is there. I don't know how I know. Steve Somsen also knows. Not that he really knows, but he's picked up on my knowing it's there.

Suddenly a particular cloud begins separating. It has the same quality as other clouds in terms of whiteness. But this one is not traveling. It's stationary, and it opens up to reveal a long, gentle slope with a slight bump—a cinder cone on the side of Mauna Kea!

The navigation at this moment seems to be out of my hands and beyond my control. I'm the one given the opportunity of feeling the emotion of the navigator not yet ready to have a complete understanding of what is happening. It is a moment of self-perspective, of one person in a vast ocean given an opportunity of looking through a window into my heritage.

I hear the crew cheering as the edge of the sun begins disappearing behind Mauna Kea. I feel their happiness, but a silence in me sets in. Venus follows the sun and touches the mountain an hour later.

It is now time to sleep, for there is nothing else to do. The sun has led us to the land. Ahead of us is our *kū'ula,* and I'm filled with a feeling of emptiness and gratitude.

But before I sleep I check on Mau. He's already asleep—something unusual for him at this time of night.

Perspective

The paths of *Hōkūleʻa* in 1976 and in 1980 are similar. Nor would we expect them to be much different since "holding close to the wind" was the criterion each time.

From a scientific point of view it's important that the two courses are so nearly parallel, for you cannot base a claim on a single event. Validation in science depends upon verification. Another investigation must yield comparable results.

Not only are the courses similar, so, too, are many of the events along the way. In 1976 *Hōkūleʻa* struggled into the wind for five days out of Maui to clear Cape Kumukahi on the island of Hawaiʻi. That problem was avoided in 1980 by leaving from Hilo; however, the canoe had to struggle for an equal number of days in stormy seas just to maintain that initial advantage. *Hōkūleʻa* 1976 sat for a week in the doldrums. *Hōkūleʻa* 1980 slowed slightly there but stalled for a week south of the equator, where on the earlier voyage it had sped along under strong trade winds.

Common to each voyage was the sighting of land on the 31st day at sea—coral islands in the Tuamotus only 20 miles apart.

Twice *Hōkūleʻa* demonstrated the windward capability of the double-hulled voyaging canoe. Twice it showed the effectiveness of the wayfinding art in locating remote islands. And the success of these voyages is strong evidence supporting the intentional voyaging hypothesis in accounting for the settling of Polynesia.

THREE COURSE LINES

Three course lines were generated in the 1980 voyage: one was constructed; a second one, measured; a third, derived.

Nainoa constructed his *reference course* long before the voyage began. It's a straight line with an elbow in it, an "ideal" course

based on the most probable conditions the navigator would expect to find along the way. It's a mental construct and has no reality other than that—a line in mind, not a course to be sailed.

The *actual course,* or "course made good," is plotted from the positions of *Hōkūleʻa* as measured by the ARGOS satellite navigating system furnished by the Scripps Institute of Oceanography, University of California at San Diego.

The *presumed course* is derived from three parameters—direction, distance, and deviation. It is a way of representing where Nainoa presumes the canoe to be.

Each day Nainoa reported his estimate of the directions to the Marquesas, Tuamotus, Societies, Cooks, and Hawaiʻi, as he perceived them to be. Aboard *Ishka* we plotted the reciprocals of those directions on Chart 526. The intersections of the five lines formed an irregular geometric figure. At the center of that figure we placed a point representing a possible position for the canoe.

The final positioning of that point, though, was influenced by two other factors. One was distance to reference islands. Nainoa derived that figure from his knowledge of the declination of stars and their altitudes at particular latitudes.

The other factor—deviation from the reference course—he determined from his continual assessment of wind strength and duration, his knowledge of and allowance for currents. He visualized how these factors might be affecting the course of the canoe and expressed that deviation from his course line in terms of "houses."

From all these uncertainties we picked a "most probable point," connecting those points of probability into a line that we call Nainoa's presumed course. The presumed course, then, is an entity based on assessments of direction, distance, and deviation. It's a documentation process and has nothing to do with actual wayfinding; its value lies in enabling us to see that which otherwise we might miss.

A LOOK AT THE COURSES

A comparison of the presumed and actual courses for the 1980 "down" voyage shows them to be close, generally within a hundred miles of each other. The presumed course is east of the actual for most of the voyage, coincident with it at the beginning and end.

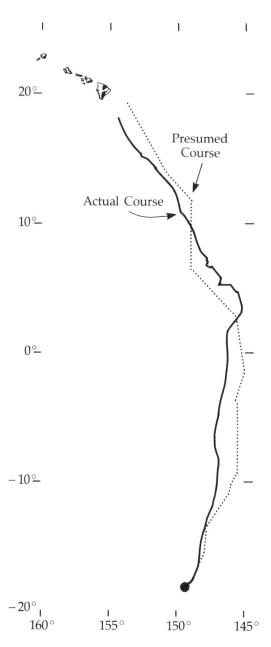

Hawai'i—Tahiti, 1980: presumed and actual courses

The courses are even closer on the "up," return, trip, never more than 60 miles apart. Again, as in the down trip, the presumed is east of the actual course in the same general region. Long after the voyage was completed, Nainoa saw the courses on paper. He was surprised and exclaimed, "That's embarrassing. Nobody'll believe us."

The 1976 voyage that Mau navigated and the 1980 that Nainoa navigated are closely parallel. Instruments were used on the 1976 return. The greatest difference between courses is found in comparison of the up and down voyages, a difference that merely shows the extent to which geography shapes strategy and the wayfinder shapes his thinking as he "holds close to the wind."

Intuitive and cognitive thinking are apparent in Nainoa's navigation. Nainoa is "more on" when he's working with intuitive factors than with cognitive ones. At least we might infer so when we translate his presumed course into elements that approximate latitude and longitude. His error (a poor term here, since the only "error" in wayfinding is missing the island) is less when he's determining longitude than latitude, that is, in determining where he is relative to the imaginary reference course (an intuitive determination) than where he is relative to the equator (a cognitive one obtained from his knowledge of star positions).

Intuition is essentially skill in guessing right, one that can be improved through training and experience. His "error" was consistently less on the up voyage, perhaps as a result of greater experience. His intuitive sense shows most clearly in his finding Hawai'i. He ordered a turn downwind at 19° N, the latitude of Mauna Kea. Turning downwind was a risk: if land had not been sighted within a reasonable time, tacking back upwind would have been required, and that's a difficult way to travel.

Analytic thinking would have had *Hōkūle'a* travel well north of the Big Island, perhaps as far as 22° N, before turning west. There is a measure of safety in such a plan: the target is larger; since the Hawaiian chain trends 1,500 miles toward the northwest, there's a greater probability of sighting islands at higher latitude.

Turning west at 19° left Nainoa no margin of error. He needed none. He knew where he was—east of Mauna Kea. Knew? How did he *know?* His decision to turn was not an analytic one, although analysis was present. Nor was it impulsive. It was intuitive, emerg-

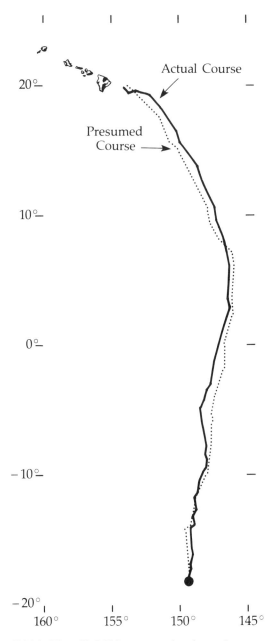

Tahiti—Hawai'i, 1980: presumed and actual courses

ing spontaneously from a lifetime's fascination with the sea, three years' intensive study of the stars, and a year's learning with Mau. Bringing most heavily to bear upon knowing when to turn was his three weeks of intensive concentration on staying oriented, in solving a problem, in finding land.

Visualizing the goal is an important part of solving a problem. Nainoa "saw" Mauna Kea long before it could be seen, just as four years earlier Mau saw Mataiva long before it appeared on an empty horizon. Nainoa recalls Mau's lesson in visualizing:

> My last lesson with Mau at Koko Head was at a time of day when we usually didn't go to study the stars. We drove to the place we normally study, got up on the wall and sat there for a while.
>
> He asked me, "Where's Tahiti?" I pointed to the compass direction.
>
> "Do you see the island?"
>
> I hesitated. I wasn't really sure what he was driving at, and I was still in my own context. "Yes," I said.
>
> "You have to remember how the islands move. If you forget that, you're lost. Let's go home."
>
> I think what Mau was saying to me is that you've got to believe to know. You've got to believe in your teachers and you've got to trust yourself. At times the principles of navigation we've set out just don't work. Not that they're wrong—it isn't that—but sometimes you just don't have the clues. If you can't believe in your intuition at such times, then you're really lost.

Nainoa derived meaning from the clues. And when the usual clues weren't there, he relied upon intuition. His knowledge was free-floating, easily available. He learned the importance of releasing his mind from striving and relying upon that intuitive sense.

> I didn't know what things I would cherish until I actually experienced them. Mau says it takes a long time to learn those things, that it's something very internal.
>
> We were sailing into the doldrums the night after Shorty's boy was born. I was anticipating the doldrums with fear—fear of get-

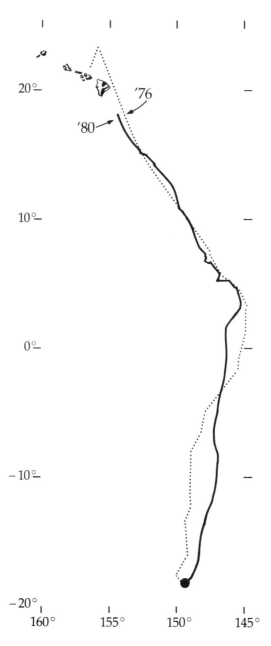

Hawai'i—Tahiti: a comparison of 1976 and 1980 courses

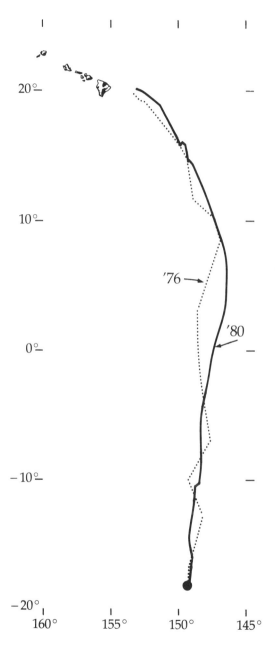

Tahiti—Hawai'i: a comparison of 1976 and 1980
courses

ting totally disoriented; but I was also really excited with the challenge. This is the place where you find out what you can take.

I can picture it so vividly. All day long it had rained. Rain was in my eyes and driving me crazy. We had no wind. I was trying to force myself to figure out where we were. But we weren't moving, so why care? All this frustration was building up inside me. Mau had always told me that you have to stay relaxed. I wasn't relaxed. In fact, I was completely the opposite and getting tired.

Thick low clouds were all around us at sunset. There was just one hole in the clouds, a little spot of blue sky. I can remember thinking, "Let's try sailing through that hole." I wasn't really thinking clearly.

Later that night it was so pitch black that you couldn't distinguish ocean from clouds. Everything was black, but we had a lot of wind. You can imagine how it is when you're trying to keep your course. All you have to position yourself is your memory. You keep the record of where you've been in your mind, all the time. It's your history. If you forget it, you're lost. Keeping thirty days in mind is difficult. And what happens when there are gaps, times you don't know where you went?

That night we were sailing fast. To where? I really wasn't sure where we were going. We continued sailing by feeling the swells. I didn't have much confidence in that because we couldn't see them even though they were high—about 12 feet. "Go steer where you like because your guess is as good as mine." Even though they were big, still it was so black they didn't even make an imprint on the horizon. You could only feel them. We had two choices—to sail, or to drop the sails and go nowhere. We continued sailing. We were going so fast for so long and in an unknown direction it was spooking me.

I gave up. I think it was because I was so tired that I just gave up forcing myself to find the clues visually. All of a sudden I felt warm, but it was raining and cold. When I gave up trying to force myself to find answers, I knew. I took command of the steering and said, "Here, we're going to go this way." When I relaxed and gave up, somehow I knew. Then there was a break in the clouds and the moon showed—exactly where I thought it was supposed to be. Even when I saw it, I wasn't surprised.

That's my most valuable moment, that one.

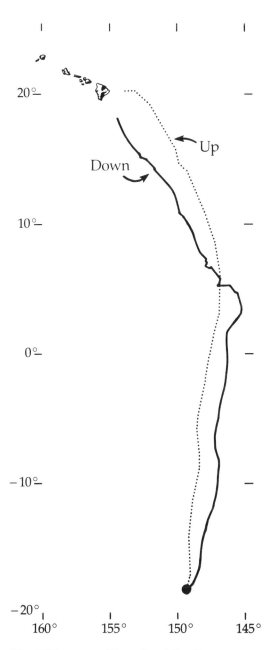

The 1980 voyages: "down" and "up" courses
compared

The Blessing

Mau was Nainoa's teacher. Never, though, was Nainoa apprenticed to Mau in the traditional master-novice sense. He was always Mau's student, an unusual one to be sure, who approached the art of wayfinding in a manner unfamiliar to Mau.

Mau and Nainoa stand together, separated only by the way they got there. Knowledge for one came through tradition; for the other, through inquiry. Two divergent paths of knowledge converged on a remote island. Each found Tahiti.

In a culture of tradition, learning comes through discipleship— through trusting the master, imitating, listening, repeating, emulating. Eventually the novice claims the ground of knowledge in which both he and the master are rooted. And on it he establishes his independence. Mau did it. He learned wayfinding from his father and his grandfather, then ventured into the South Pacific without previous knowledge of that route.

No way, though, was there for Nainoa fully to understand traditional navigation. He arrived by a different route. By inquiry. He chose to be puzzled. He invented what he needed in order to discover, borrowing from Mau that which was freely given. His originality is expressed in a wayfinding system uniquely his own.

"You're too old to learn," Mau told him, "You should have started when you were five." The early-starting apprentice may acquire a certain naturalness, both through working with the master and in participating in corporate retrospection. But that way was not open to Nainoa. He learned by studying. His advantage was a machine—logical, sequential analysis—a way of catching up on time.

Wayfinding is a set of principles. An art. And at the center of the circle of sea and sky is the wayfinder practicing the art, trusting mind and senses within a cognitive structure to read and interpret nature's signs along the way as the means for maintaining continuous orientation to a remote, intended destination.

Full colleague status is conferred upon the Carolinian novice in the act of "uncovering the bowl," competence being recognized in the privilege of eating with other navigators.

Mau danced and sang at a *lūʻau* celebrating the arrival of *Hōkūleʻa* in Tahiti. Then, at the moment that was right for him he went to Nainoa's family—grandmother, mother, father, sister, and brother—greeting each and saying, "You are my sister," or "You are my brother," welcoming each into his own family.

Happy with Nainoa's success, he turned to his special student and said, "Now you know all there is to know."

Nainoa lowered his head, for he was touched with the blessing of the master.

Mau smiled and added, "But it will be twenty years before you see."

CREW MEMBERS ON *HŌKŪLEʻA* 1976, 1977, 1978, 1980

HAWAIʻI-TAHITI, 1976

Clifford Ah Mow
Shorty Bertelmann
Ben Finney
Tommy Holmes
Sam Kalalau
Boogie Kalama
Kawika Kapahulehua
Buffalo Keaulana

John Kruse
Dukie Kauhulu
David Lewis
Dave Lyman
Mau Piailug
Billy Richards
Rodo Williams

TAHITI-HAWAIʻI, 1976

Snake Ah Hee
Andy Espirto
Kawika Kapahulehua
Mel Kinney
Kainoa Lee
Kimo Lyman
Gordon Piʻianaiʻa

Leonard Puputauiki
Penny Rawlins
Keani Reiner
Nainoa Thompson
Makaʻala Yates
Ben Young

KEALAIKAHIKI, 1977

Bert Barber
Teene Froiseth
Sam Kaʻai
Sam Kalalau
John Kruse
Dave Lyman
Kimo Lyman

Jerry Muller
Gordon Piʻianaiʻa
Norman Piʻianaiʻa
Nainoa Thompson
Mike Tongg
Makaʻala Yates

HAWAIʻI-TAHITI, 1978

Snake Ah Hee
Eddie Aikau
Charman Akina
Wedemeyer Au
Bruce Blankenfeld
Kilila Hugho
Sam Kaʻai
John Kruse

Dave Lyman
Marion Lyman
Buddy McGuire
Norman Piʻianaiʻa
Leon Sterling
Curt Sumida
Tava Taupu
Nainoa Thompson

HAWAIʻI-TAHITI, 1980

Pat Aiu
Chad Baybayan
Shorty Bertelmann
Harry Ho
Sam Kaʻai
Buddy McGuire
Marion Lyman-Mersereau

Mau Piailug
Gordon Piʻianaiʻa
Steve Somsen
Jo-Anne Sterling
Leon Sterling
Tava Taupu
Nainoa Thompson

TAHITI-HAWAIʻI, 1980

Snake Ah Hee
Wedemeyer Au
Chad Baybayan
Bruce Blankenfeld
John Kruse
Kainoa Lee
Kimo Lyman

Gordon Piʻianaiʻa
Mau Piailug
Steve Somsen
Leon Sterling
Nainoa Thompson
Michael Tongg
Nathan Wong

FOR FURTHER READING

Baker, R. R. *Human Navigation and the Sixth Sense*. New York: Simon and Schuster, 1981.

Bruner, J. S. *On Knowing: Essays for the Left Hand*. Cambridge: Harvard University Press, 1962.

Buck, P. H. (Te Rangi Hiroa). *Vikings of the Sunrise*. New York: Lippincott, 1938.

Campbell, J. *Grammatical Man*. New York: Simon and Schuster, 1982.

Davidson, Graham R. Cognitive Mapping Features of Micronesian Navigation Systems. In *Thinking—The Expanding Frontier*, edited by W. Maxwell. Hillsdale, NJ: L. Erlbaum Assocs., 1983.

Downs, R., and D. Stea. *Maps in Minds: Reflections on Cognitive Mapping*. New York: Harper & Row, 1977.

Emory, Kenneth P. Coming of the Polynesians. *National Geographic* 146 (1974) no. 6: 732–746.

Finney, B. R. New Perspectives on Polynesian Voyaging. In *Polynesian Culture History*, edited by G. A. Highland. Honolulu: Bishop Museum Press, 1967.

———. *Hokule'a: The Way to Tahiti*. New York: Dodd, Mead & Co., 1979.

Gardner, M. *Frames of Mind: The Theory of Multiple Intelligences*. New York: Basic Books, 1983.

Gelwick, R. *The Way of Discovery*. Oxford: Oxford University Press, 1977.

Gladwin, T. *East Is a Big Bird*. Cambridge: Harvard University Press, 1970.

Jennings, J. D. *The Prehistory of Polynesia*. Cambridge: Harvard University Press, 1979.

Johnson, R. K. *Na Inoa Hoku*. Honolulu: Topgallant Press, 1975.

Kane, Herb Kawainui. The Pathfinders. *National Geographic* 146 (1974) no. 6: 756–783.

———. A Canoe Helps Hawaii Recapture Her Past. *National Geographic* 149 (1976) no. 4: 468–489.

Kloeckner, P., J. M. Williams, and T. C. Williams. Radar and Visual Observations of Transpacific Migrants. *Hawaii Audubon Soc. Journ.* 42 (1982). Honolulu.

Kyselka, W., and G. W. Bunton. *Polynesian Stars and Men*. Honolulu: Bishop Museum Science Center, 1969.

Kyselka, W., and R. Lanterman. *North Star to Southern Cross*. Honolulu: University of Hawaii Press, 1976.

Lewis, David. *We, the Navigators*. Honolulu: The University Press of Hawaii, 1972.

———. Wind, Wave, Star, and Bird. *National Geographic* 146 (1974) no. 6: 747–755.

———. *Hokule'a* Follows the Stars to Tahiti. *National Geographic* 150 (1976) no. 4: 512–537.

Lindo, C. K., ed. *Polynesian Seafaring Heritage*. Honolulu: Polynesian Voyaging Society/Kamehameha Schools, 1980.

Lipman, V. The Young Man and the Sea. *Honolulu* 15 (November 1980): 68–74.

Maxwell, William, ed. *Thinking—the Expanding Frontier*. Philadelphia: The Franklin Institute Press, 1983.

Moorehead, Alan. *Darwin and the Beagle*. New York: Harper & Row, 1969.

Motteler, Lee S. *Pacific Island Names*. Honolulu: Bishop Museum Press, 1986.

Ong, W. J. *Orality and Literacy*. London and New York: Methuen, 1982.

Polanyi, M. *Personal Knowledge*. Chicago: University of Chicago Press, 1958.

Polanyi, M., and Harry Prosch. *Meaning*. Chicago: University of Chicago Press, 1975.

Polya, G. *How to Solve It*. Princeton: Princeton University Press, 1945.

INDEX

References to maps are in boldface.

Achernar. *See* Stars
Acrux. *See* Stars
Adz, 143, 192
Alaska, 13, 56, 108
Ala Wai: Channel, 31; Harbor, 31
Aldebaran. *See* Stars
'Alenuihāhā Channel, 23, 108–110
"Alex." *See* Stars
Alioth. *See* Stars
Alkaid. *See* Stars
Alpha Centauri. *See* Stars
Altair. *See* Stars
Antares. *See* Stars
Aquarius (Water Carrier). *See* Constellations
Arcturus/Hōkūle'a. *See* Stars
Argo Navis (Jason's ship). *See* Constellations
Argos. *See* Satellite
Aries (Ram). *See* Constellations
Asia, 11, 13, 14, 84, 88, 98
Atria. *See* Stars
Australia, 13
Avior. *See* Stars

BBC, 85–89
Bernice P. Bishop Museum and Planetarium,
    ix, x, 3, 4, 19, 22, 27, 30, 32, 34, 35, 37,
    44, 45, 47, 56, 61
Beta Centauri. *See* Stars
Betelgeuse. *See* Stars
Big Dipper/*Nā-hiku. See* Star Groups
Birds, 13, 95, 96, 101, 159, 181, 194, 213,
    216, 219, 220; blue-masked boobie, 130;
    brown boobie, 216; dove/*manu kū,* 194,
    211, 215, 219; golden plover, 13; noddy
    tern/*noio,* 97, 188, 194; ring-necked mal-
    lard, 216; ruddy turnstone, 13; sander-
    ling, 13; wandering tattler, 13; white
    tropic bird/*koa'e kea,* 188, 215

Cancer (Crab). *See* Constellations
Canis Major (Big Dog). *See* Constellations
Canoe building, 33–34

Canopus. *See* Stars
Cape Kumukahi, 20, 120, 125, 126, 130,
    132, 223
Capella. *See* Stars
Capricornus (Goat). *See* Constellations
Carina (Keel). *See* Constellations
Caroline Island, 159, 182
Caroline Islands, 11, 17, 84, 90, 199
Castor. *See* Stars
Celestial pole: north, 54, 163; south, 41, 55
Celestial sphere, 37–39 passim
Clouds: as aids to navigation, 210; as indica-
    tors of proximity of land, 101, 104, 219,
    221; as wind and weather predictors, 110,
    119, 120, 145, 157, 165, 178, 184, 191,
    206, 208, 211, 213, 219; spinning, 149.
    See also "Smoke"
Coast Guard. *See* United States Coast Guard
Constellations, **36, 48, 50–52, 54–57;**
    Aquarius, 196; Argo Navis, 47; Aries, 43,
    47, 215; Cancer, 47; Canis Major, 27;
    Capricornus, 91; Carina, 47; Corona
    Borealis, 9; Corvus, 61, 196; Draco, 165;
    Eridanus, 49; Gemini, 47; Hydra, 49;
    Leo, 47, 49, 52, 64; Libra, 43; Musca,
    165; Orion, 47–49, 53, 56, 64; Pegasus,
    52; Pisces, 47; Puppis, 47; Sagittarius, 50,
    91, 108; Scorpius, 50, 109, 196, 218;
    Southern Cross, 22, 26, 27, 40, 41, 44,
    49–53 passim, 56, 108, 141, 143, 146,
    147, 166, 173, 187, 206, 214–218 pas-
    sim; Taurus, 47, 48; Ursa Minor, 61, 141,
    173; Vela, 47; Virgo, 3, 47
Cook, Captain James, 12, 108, 201
Cook Islands, 35, 65, 137, 159, 171
Cor Caroli. *See* Stars
Corona Borealis (Northern Crown). *See* Con-
    stellations
Corvus (Crow). *See* Constellations
Courses: actual and presumed, 225–232 pas-
    sim, **226, 228;** comparison of 1976 and
    1980 voyages, 223, **230, 231;** reference

241

course, 98, 103, 139, 141, 146–171 passim, 182, 211, 223, 225; referred to as the "line," 131, 143, 159, 181, 188, 194, 225

Currents, 98, 157, 181, 182, 188; as indicators of proximity of land, 104; countercurrent, 98, 146–149 passim, 163; south equatorial, 184, 186

Cyclonic disturbances, 98

Darwin, Charles, 201

Deneb. *See* Stars

Departure ceremony, 117–119, 160, 206

Diamond Head, 31

Doldrums, 98, 129, 146–173 passim, 179, 223, 229

Draco (Dragon). *See* Constellations

Drake, Sir Francis, 86

Drift, 129, 134, 144, 151, 154, 157, 161, 181. *See also* Currents

Dubhe. *See* Stars

Easter Island, 11, 12

Easting, 23, 147

Ecliptic, 38, 39

Ellice Islands, 11

El Niño, 184

Equator: terrestrial, 19, 27, 38, 43, 44, 47, 53, 70, 85, 98, 159, 165–173 passim, 179, 188, 211, 223; celestial, 38, 48

Equinox, vernal, 70, 135, 179

Eridanus (River). *See* Constellations

Escort vessel: as possible distraction, 173; choice of, 104; curtailment of radio communication due to engine failure, 153–155

False Cross. *See* Star Groups

Fishing, 139, 151, 191–192, 213; *ahi*, 135, 141, 191, 192, 213; *aku*, 192, 213; *kawakawa*, 213; *mahimahi*, 192, 193, 213; *ono*, 192; shark, 182, 185

Fishhooks, 151, 188

Flint Island, 159

Gacrux. *See* Stars

Gemini (Twins). *See* Constellations

Gienah. *See* Stars

Gilbert Islands, 11

Halley, Sir Edmund, 201

Hāmākua Coast, 110–115 passim, **132**, 151, 218

Hamal. *See* Stars

Hawai'i Island, 24–26, 32, 110–123 passim, **124, 132**, 159, 215–220 passim, 223, 227

Hawaiian Islands, as target for navigator, 227

Hilo, 103, 107–110 passim, 117–139 passim, **124, 132, 136**, 163, 186, 205, 223

Hōkūle'a (canoe), construction of, 15; description of, 15, 17, 73, 74, 76, 78, 79, 133, 149, 156, 160, 165, 166, 196, 223; diagram of, 74; educational use of, 105, 139; in distress, 17, 31, 110–116; in drydock, 78–81; provisioning of, 119, 182, 213; safety equipment aboard, 112, 131, 176; sea trials of, 17; tonnage of, 31, 78, 133, 155, 212. *See also* Steering Sweep

Hōkūle'a (star). *See* Stars: Arcturus

Honolulu, **19, 124, 136**

"Houses," 97, 130, 131, 135–159 passim, 181, 188, 194, 206–220 passim. *See also* Courses; Star Compass

Hydra (Sea Serpent). *See* Constellations

Ice Age, 13

Intertropical Convergence Zone, 98. *See also* Trade Winds

Ishka. See Escort Vessel

Japan, 11, 92

Jupiter. *See* Planets

Kaho'olawe Island, **19**, 23, **25**

Kapingamarangi Island, 30

Kappa Verlorum. *See* Stars

Kaua'i Channel, 17

Kaua'i Island, 17, **19**, 139, 219

Kawaiaha'o Church, 32, 105–108, 112

Kawaihae, 116, **132**

Kawakawa. See Fishing

Kealaikahiki Experiment, 3, 23–27, 117, 130, 191

Kochab. *See* Stars

Kona, 26, **131**

Kon Tiki, 12, 198

Kualoa, 15

Lāna'i Island, 23

Latitude, 35, 47–57 passim, 62, 101, 139, 147, 157, 158, 162, 169, 171, 189, 227; determination of, 42–45, 173, 194

Leo (Lion). *See* Constellations

Libra (Balance or Scales). *See* Constellations

Longitude, 101, 142, 157, 159, 162; related to Greenwich, 169, 227

Magellanic Clouds. *See* Star Groups

Makatea Island, 198, 199

Mariana Islands, 14, 84. *See also* Micronesia
Marquesas Islands, 13, **102,** 105, **124, 136,** 159, 163, 171, 173, 182
Mars. *See* Planets
Marshall Islands, 11
Mataiva Island, 20, 188, 194, 197, 198, 229
Matavai Bay, 201, 205
Maui Island, 19, 23, 105, 108, 109, 178, 219, 223
Mauna Kea, 11, 116, 119, 122, **132,** 218, 219, 221, 222, 227, 229
Mauna Loa, 11, 24, 119, **132**
Megrez. *See* Stars
Melanesia, 11
Menkent. *See* Stars
Merak. *See* Stars
Meridian, 27–29 passim, 38, 39, 43, 44, 49, 51
Miaplacidus. *See* Stars
Micronesia, 11, 19. *See also* Saipan; Satawal
Midway Island, 125
Milky Way. *See* Star Groups
Mintaka. *See* Constellations: Orion; Stars
Mira. *See* Stars
Mirzam. *See* Constellations: Canis Major; Stars
Moloka'i Channel, ix, 31, 62, 69, 83
Moloka'i Island, **19, 24, 25,** 31, 76, 107, 110
Moon: as aid in determining direction, 3, 4, 41, 98, 143, 151, 159, 206, 209; phases of, 129. *See also* Sun
Mo'orea Island, 202. *See also* Society Islands; Tahiti
Musca (Fly). *See* Constellations

Navi. *See* Stars
New Guinea, 13
New Zealand, 12
North pole, 42, 56, 147–148

O'ahu Island, **19,** 31, 62, 64, 77, 88, 119–121 passim
Obtuse Triangle. *See* Star Groups
Oceania, **10,** 11, 88
Omega Centauri Cluster. *See* Star Groups
Orion (Hunter). *See* Constellations

Pacific Ocean: temperature measurement of, 184
Pailolo Channel, 108
Panama, 11
Pape'ete, 20, **34,** 148, 185, 199–203. *See also* Society Islands; Tahiti

Pegasus (Winged Horse). *See* Constellations
Phecda. *See* Stars
Philippine Islands, 11
Physician, aboard *Hōkūle'a,* 128, 168, 213
Pisces (Fishes). *See* Constellations
Planets: as aids in determination of direction, 23, 151; as "Wanderers," 3; conjunction of Jupiter and Mars, 66; of Jupiter, Mars, and Saturn, 139; transit of Venus, 201
Pleiades (Cluster of Little Eyes)/*Nā-huihui-a-Makali'i. See* Star Groups
Point Reyes, CA, 138
Point Venus, 201, 205
Polaris (North Star)/*Hōkūpa'a. See* Stars
Pollux. *See* Stars
Polynesia, 11, 52; settlement of, 12–14
Polynesian Triangle, **10,** 12
Polynesian Voyaging Society, xi, 14, 15, 17, 23, 37, 63, 104, 105, 115, 148, 184
Procyon. *See* Stars
Puppis (Stern). *See* Constellations

Radio KMI, 137, 138, 148, 151
Radio Mahina, x, 199
Radio Station KCCN, 138–142, 151
Radio WWVH, 178
Rangiroa Island, **124, 136,** 196, 197. *See also* Tuamotu Islands
Raroia Island, 198
Regulus. *See* Constellations: Leo; Stars
Rigel. *See* Constellations: Orion; Stars

Sabik. *See* Stars
Sagittarius (Archer). *See* Constellations
Saipan, 59, 62, 84. *See also* Micronesia
Samoa, 9, 14, 35
Santa Cruz Island, 37
Satawal Island, 17, 20, 59, 62, 65, 214. *See also* Micronesia
Satellite, 157, 162, 184, 225
Saturn. *See* Planets
Scorpius (Maui's Fishhook). *See* Constellations
Scripps Institute of Oceanography, 157, 225
Shedar. *See* Stars
Sheratan. *See* Stars
Shipboard routine, 175–177, 199, 213; preparation for sighting land, 195–196; water consumption, 182. *See also* Fishing
Siberia, 13
Singapore, 11, 81–93 passim
Sirius/*A'a. See* Stars
"Smoke," 64–66, 69, 74, 120, 191. *See also* Clouds
Society Islands, 159, 171. *See also* Pape'ete; Tahiti

South America, 12

South Point/*Ka Lae*, **19, 25,** 125, 128, **132,** 215, 219

Southern Cross (Crux)/*Newa. See* Constellations

Spica. *See* Stars

Squall: as source of fresh water, 181, 189; as wind indicator, 137, 145, 157, 158

Stars, **36, 40, 48–57;** Achernar, 28, 49; Acrux, 44, 50; Aldebaran, 48; "Alex," 146; Alioth, 29, 44, 53, 189, 194; Alkaid, 28, 29, 163; Alpha Centauri, 50, 141, 173, 187, 215; Altair, 44, 50, 61, 70; Antares, 27, 76, 85; Arcturus, 13, 16, 27, 29, 42, 43, 49, 51, 53, 57, 61, 70, 78; Atria, 146, 165, 215; Avior, 27–29 passim, 49, 147; Beta Centauri, 50, 147, 173, 187, 215; Betelgeuse, 28; Canopus, 27, 41, 44, 47, 52, 53, 97, 173; Capella, 53; Castor, 53; Cor Caroli, 29, 44, 53; culmination of, 39, 44; Deneb, 50; Dubhe, 29, 50, 189, 194; Gacrux, 44, 50; Gienah, 27, 53; Hamal, 47, 215; Kappa Velorum, 49; Kochab, 29, 52, 165, 189; Megrez, 28, 194; Menkent, 147; Merak, 49, 189, 194; Miaplacidus, 147, 165; Mintaka, 48, 52, 53, 85; Mira, 159; Mirzam, 41, 47, 53, 173; mythical distribution of, 9; Navi, 28; Phecda, 189, 194; Polaris, 19, 27, 40, 42, 43, 50, 51, 52, 56, 61, 70, 85, 146, 163, 206, 215, 218; Pollux, 53; Procyon, 28; Regulus, 27, 49, 154; Rigel, 49, 52; Sabik, 53; Shedar, 29; Sheratan, 47, 215; Sirius, 28, 41–43 passim, 47, 48, 53, 61; Spica, 3, 9, 27, 49, 52, 61; "storm stars," 61, 62; synchronous rising and setting, 20, 22, 44, 45, 49, 53, 95, 173; Vega, 44, 50, 61; "Willy Star," 141; zenith, 42, 85, 173; Zubenelgenubi, 53. *See also* Constellations; Meridian; Star Compass; Star Groups; Star Pairs

Star Compass, 38, 39, 63, 95, 96, 102

Star Groups: Big Dipper, 9, 47, 49–53 passim, 85, 173; False Cross, 27, 28, 47, 50, 51; Magellanic Clouds, 53; Milky Way, 50, 143, 185, 218; Obtuse Triangle, 194; Omega Centauri Cluster, 185; Pleiades, 9, 48, 185

Star Pairs, 40, 44

Steering sweep, 72, 75, 77–78, 94, 133, 144, 159, 203, 211

Sun/*Lā*, 42; as aid in determining direction, 39, 98, 143, 167, 175, 213–215 passim; as aid in instrumental navigation, 26, 178–

179; "House of,"/*Haleakalā*, 92; and moon relationship, 4, 41–41, 209; position in galaxy, 185; relationship with Star Compass, 95, 97

Swells, as navigational aids, 70, 97, 145, 146, 149, 151–161 passim, 167, 175, 182, 186, 194, 210–213 passim, 220, 232

Tahiti, 9, 11, 13–20 passim, 23, 229, 230; latitude of, 29, 42, 44; problems of navigation to and from, 98–102; simulated voyage to, 47–58; 1976 voyage to, 20; 1980 voyage to, 125–203; return voyage from, 205–222. *See also* Society Islands

Takapoto Island, 98, **124,** 141

Tasmania, 13

Taurus (Bull). *See* Constellations

Teti'aroa Island, 201, 206

Tevake, 37

Tikehau Island, 197

Tokelau Island, 11

Tonga, 14, 35, 48, 56

Trade Winds, 78, 97, 98, 104, 210, 213; convergence of, 149, 152, 191; southeast, 156, 184, 196

Transponder, 104, 157, 184. *See also* Satellite

Tuamotu Islands, 11, 13, 14, 19, 20, 26, 53, 98, 141, 159, 163, 171, 173, 188, 194, 195, 223. *See also* Society Islands

Tubuai-Austral Islands, 14

United States Coast Guard, Honolulu Communication Station (COMSTA) and Rescue, 111–115, 125, 130, 135, 151, 155, 156, 161

University of Hawaii, ix, 5, 157

'Upolo Point, 23, **132**

Ursa Minor (Little Dipper). *See* Constellations

Vega. *See* Stars

Vela (Sail). *See* Constellations

Venus. *See* Planets

Virgo (Virgin). *See* Constellations

Vostok Island, 159

Waikiki, 76

Wake Island, 14

"Willy Star." *See* Stars

Windward landfall, necessity for, 101

Wrap-around winds, 26

Zenith, 53, 56, 85. *See also* Stars

Zodiac, 38

Zubenelgenubi. *See* Stars